Learn How to Protect & Restore Yourself from Negative Energy

SADANAND PUJARI

Published by SADANAND PUJARI, 2024.

Also by SADANAND PUJARI

Master The Psychology Of Weight Loss Via Hypnosis Build Healthy Sleep Habits Learn The Art Of Meditation Improve People Management And Build Employee Engagement
Content Marketing Masterclass Create Content That Sells Cyber Security For Normal People Protect Yourself Online Kanban Fundamentals How To Become Insanely Productive
Positive Psychology Art Therapy: Certified Training Bookkeeping In Quickbooks Online (Bookkeeping & Accounting)
Business Impact of Digital Transformation Technologies Learn How to Protect & Restore Yourself from Negative Energy

Table of Contents

Copyright

Learn How to Protect & Restore Yourself from Negative Energy

Copyright © **SADANAND PUJARI**, 2024

Cover design by **SADANAND PUJARI**

All rights reserved. No part of this publication may be reproduced, stored in a retrieval system, or transmitted in any form or by any means electronic, mechanical, photocopy, recording, or any other except for brief quotations, not to exceed 400 words, without the prior permission of the publisher.

First published in 2024 by

SADANAND PUJARI

About

For years I've been asked "How do you protect yourself?" - energetically speaking - given the number of healing sessions and student attunement ceremonies I do each week. In response to that, I found myself explaining in bits & pieces here and there, and only to those who asked.

Whilst I teach simple protection steps in most of my Books, it became apparent that I needed to look closely at my routine (which has just become second-nature over time), document it, and share it with others. I've not just done this "deep dive" into protection for my fellow Reki practitioners and energy healers, but also for those who work in emotionally demanding jobs (such as healthcare workers) and for those who are really sensitive to the negative energy of others (such as empaths) so here we are!

These techniques are ones I use everyday in what I call Energetic Protection. In this book, you'll learn what energy is and how you fit into the Energy Field, how to engage and listen to your intuition, identify the source of the negativity, how to use specific tools and techniques for protection, how to restore your energy, as well go through my step-by-step process in order to safeguard that beautiful energy of yours!

By the end of our journey together, you'll be able to implement protection steps that help preserve and restore your energy levels so you can live your best life, every day.

Chapter - 1

One, human energy fields. Measuring the human energy output. With progress in modern science, we're becoming more and more aware that the human organism is not just a physical structure made up of molecules, that we are electrochemical and electromagnetic beings made up of energy fields. Our bodies may appear to be solid and opaque, but if we could magnify the cells, molecules and atoms of which we are composed, we would see that at the most fundamental level, we are made up of energy, of electrochemical and electromagnetic activity that is constantly going on in our bodies. If electricity is the force behind the electromagnetic energy fields, magnetism is the direction giving aspect of that force.

The magnetic aspect of our energy fields has to do with our functioning in the physical world. For example, it is what keeps us upright. There is increasing scientific evidence for this view of human energy fields. For years, scientists have been able to detect the energy emitted by the body by measuring skin potentials in order to measure the electrical output of various organs. Researchers placed electrodes on the skin. To measure the electrical output of the brain, for example, electrodes are placed on the forehead and the scalp in the cerebral area. Similarly, the electrocardiogram measures the electrical output of the heart through electrodes placed on the skin of the chest wall, the polygraph or lie detector measures, the changes in the electrical potential of the skin or the galvanic skin resistance.

4

In all these cases, we're not sure exactly what is being measured, but we do know that we are measuring a form of radiation. We would not be able to measure it if it were not radiant or electromagnetic energy. But because all these measurements are taken using skin potentials, we're not really accurately measuring the output of the organism itself. We get interference from the skin that lies between our instruments and the organ whose output is being measured. We now have a better method for measuring the electromagnetic output of the body instead of using skin potentials. We can measure the electromagnetic forces around the body directly.

This has to be done under special conditions with extremely sensitive instruments. Originally, this type of measurement was done in a shielded room so that all the electromagnetic noise from such sources as the electrical equipment in the building, power lines in the street and atmospheric disturbances would be filtered out. The instrument used to take these very sensitive measurements is known as the superconducting quantum interference device or the squid. Originally, the squid was set up in a special shielded room 20 feet underground at the Massachusetts Institute of Technology.

However, over the last several years, the device has been improved to the point that for some purposes it does not need to be shielded anymore, although it is, of course, still preferable to use such a device in a place where there is little electrical interference. This electromagnetic output of the body is measured in a unit of magnetism known as the gas, of course, the earth itself radiates electromagnetic energy. Every particle on earth, even though it may appear solid and stationary to us, has continual activity taking place within it. It looks solid and dense because the energy is of high frequency and low amplitude. The electromagnetic output of the earth is on average one 1/2 goss'.

By comparison, the electromagnetic output of the human body is one billionth of one half. This very tiny uproar can be measured by the squid, so you can see what an extremely sensitive instrument it is. By measuring skin, potential scientists have found that there are both alternating currents and direct currents coming from the body. Such currents arise from the migration of electrically charged particles or ions in the body tissues and fluids. These AC DC currents give rise to corresponding magnetic fields. At present, there is only one system of the human body from which an electromagnetic output has not been measured. The blood system.

Interestingly, this is consistent with what I have observed about the blood system, which I like to compare to a system of freeways, roads, side streets with the blood itself, like a trucking company that needs to have its trucks loaded and unloaded so that the ingredients can be distributed to the tissues and organs. of course, the trucks themselves might have electrical components, but as long as they're not interacting with each other, they would not emit radiation sufficient to measure. I'm not sure that the blood does not have some electrical output of its own arising from what is happening within the blood system itself.

But if this app does exist, it has not been measured, at least not with the squid. Modern medicine loves to take blood samples from patients to diagnose what is wrong with them, if we think of the blood system as a trucking company. We can see the fallacy in this approach. The nutrients and other substances found in the blood are not of primary importance. What matters is whether there is a crew at the other end to load and unload the trucks when they arrive at their destination. We shall later examine in some detail this area of assimilation. Besides the energy outputs that have been measured outside the body, there are other subtle forces acting within the body that are not yet understood by science.

The Soviet researcher, Dr. Alexandre Dubrow, has found that during mitosis or the splitting of cells, there is photon radiation from the cells. As you know, photons are particle waves of light, this radiation produces a dim glow, which we might call bioluminescence. The photon emissions produced by the cells in our bodies are in the ultraviolet frequencies beyond what we know as the visible spectrum. All the trillions of cells in our bodies are emitting such photons from one to another. This emission does not stop at the skin surface, for the skin is also made up of cells. Perhaps this discovery helps us to understand some of the ancient references to light in the sacred texts.

The Christian scriptures say you are light, and if therefore then I am single, their whole body shall be full of light. The meaning of that fascinating statement may not be purely symbolic or philosophical in Egyptian religion, a related image, the so-called Horus, has been looked upon as the eye symbolizing health. Well, what is meant by the single eye, as long as we see positive and negative as two separate things. There is no light. If you have a positive energy field and a negative energy field and they do not merge, there's no current. So if you still see something out of your right eye that is different from what you see with your left eye, there is an unbalanced condition. You are not perceiving things in their wholeness. So you are not in a healthy state.

We know that in the human body, fluids are suspended in crystals as those cells or crystalline substances. In another series of Soviet experiments replicated thousands of times, researchers put single cells in each of two glass test tubes. They first measured the electronic potential of each cell and its biochemical composition. The two test tubes were then placed next to each other and nothing happened. The experimenter is next injected into one of the test tubes, substances that would disturb the physiological state of the single cell so that it would become different electronically and biochemically from the other, making it, in effect, a disease cell.

As long as the cells were in the glass test tubes, nothing happened. The sea continued to be seized and the healthy cells continued to be healthy. The scientists then caught it between the cells, actually, they put the cells in test tubes. Immediately, they reported there was what they call a mirror image effect, within seconds, the healthy cells started to show symptoms similar to those of the disease cells. Do and his colleagues were able to measure at that time ultraviolet photo and transference from one cell to the other. We know then that the crystalline part of our cellular structure is emitting photons in the ultraviolet wavelengths. Your researchers have observed that during mitosis, the cell emits not only light, but also very high frequency sound.

They found that it is possible to measure such ultrasonic sound within the body wherever there is light. Then there is also sound. Of course, such sound goes beyond the frequencies that we can hear. Eventually, we will be able to hear the sounds of our body by amplifying and translating them so that they become perceptible to our senses. And we may then be able to diagnose those signals as one means of detecting illness. Knowledge that was once thought of as a trick is now becoming exothermic, it is becoming scientific knowledge. I believe that within the next five or 10 years, you may well be able to step into an instrument, be surrounded by an electrostatic field and immediately see a display on screens of what is happening in your body, in living colors, and you will see or hear the sound of your own body.

If this can be amplified and made visible and audible to us, diagnostics will become much easier because as we shall see later on, it is possible to tell a great deal about the state of a person's health from the patterns of ammunition and absorption in his or her energy fields. Educating the senses. If we realize that the human body is surrounded by energy fuels that can be detected by sensitive instruments like the squid, we will have a better understanding of what is meant by the aura. For many people, the aura has acquired a metaphysical meaning, and it was often felt that the aura is not really there or that it can be seen only by very highly developed, sensitive spiritual beings. This is a fallacy.

What prevents you from seeing the aura is the fact that your eyesight is not properly educated. If you start educating your eyes, which you will learn to do in Chapter four, you will have a greater ability to perceive the activity taking place in so-called material objects. I've seen people who are absolutely non-spiritual, develop their physical vision properly and learn to see energy fields around others. I must emphasize that with proper Chapter of your eyesight, you can observe energy fields emanating not only from the human body, but also from all material substances, including plants and inanimate matter. It is not an insult to the higher species to say that a plant or a rock can have an energy field. The human body is made up of exactly the same materials as animals, vegetables and minerals.

All the elements in our bodies are the same as elements that can be found in the crust and the atmosphere of the Earth. The only difference is that we have a higher level of activity within our bodies that gives us a higher energy input and output and therefore we have a higher level of consciousness. When you expand your energy, you automatically go beyond the denser state and things become subtler, clearer and easier to perceive with the senses. We might make an analogy between two substances such as water and molasses. Both are fluid, but the molasses is thick, dense and practically opaque, whereas water is free and clear and flowing. The same thing is true of the human body in relation to the rest of the world.

We seem to be more flexible, more expendable, and therefore we have a capacity for higher consciousness.

We are able to radiate more and further and we are correspondingly more sensitive to things further beyond our own means. Some esoteric riders proclaim that in order to pursue what we call God the universal, the environment beyond the human environment, one has to have an extra sense. We have enough trouble with the five senses we've got, so let's not make it more difficult by adding another one to the list, you do not have to be psychic as every book on earth seems to tell you, in order to see the energy fields around human beings. So get away from the idea that you have to be a special person to do it. We are living in a three dimensional world and beyond our three dimensional world, there exists a multi dimensional world which we call the universe.

When we speak of certain energy fields as we have measured them on planet Earth, we have to realize that is only how we have perceived them in the human environment, in Earth's environment and in our own solar system. Beyond that, we really do not know in what form the energy or occurs. Some people often actually receive something from those planes beyond the human environment, our planet's environment, our solar system and even our galaxy. This experience is multidimensional and it is impossible to recount such experiences in three dimensional language. But do not get the mistaken idea that you do not use your five senses for such perception, your five senses are the receptors for any visual, auditory, tactile, olfactory and gustatory images that you perceive.

No matter what form such images may represent on a multidimensional plane, once these images have been perceived by the senses of the physical body, they're translated into physiological events in this three dimensional world. Although we are limited to our five senses, they can be greatly expanded and made much more sensitive. We're capable of becoming hyper aesthetic or hypersensitive through our five senses. The state expands our capacity to tune in and enables us to go beyond our own immediate environment.

Note the similarity between in tune with and intuitive, this is not a mysterious state beyond our understanding, it can be translated into the physical because we use our physical bodies and our senses for it. Such hyper static states can be evoked by hypnotic suggestion under normal circumstances, a person might not be able to perceive a certain stimulus with his or her senses. But through hypnosis, it is possible to increase the sensitivity of his or her perception to a higher level. In one experiment, for example, a subject could read a book held five feet in front of him, but if it was held at a much greater distance away, he could no longer be. The subject was then hypnotized and given special opaque glasses that had mirrors on the insides of the glass so they could look.

Chapter - 2

Can be measured by the squid, so you can see what an extremely sensitive instrument that is. By measuring skin, potential scientists have found that there are both alternating currents and direct currents coming from the body. Such currents arise from the migration of electrically charged particles or ions in the body tissues and fluids. These AC DC currents give rise to corresponding magnetic fields. At present, there is only one system of the human body from which an electromagnetic output has not been measured. The blood system. Interestingly, this is consistent with what I have observed about the blood system, which I like to compare to a system of freeways, roads, side streets with the blood itself, like a trucking company that needs to have its trucks loaded and unloaded so that the ingredients can be distributed to the tissues and organs.

Of course, the trucks themselves might have electrical components, but as long as they're not interacting with each other, they would not emit radiation sufficient to measure. I'm not sure that the blood does not have some electrical output of its own arising from what is happening within the blood system itself. But if this app does exist, it has not been measured, at least not with the squid. Modern medicine loves to take blood samples from patients to diagnose what is wrong with them, if we think of the blood system as a trucking company. We can see the fallacy in this approach. The nutrients and other substances found in the blood are not of primary importance.

What matters is whether there is a crew at the other end to load and unload the trucks when they arrive at their destination. We shall later examine in some detail this area of assimilation. Besides the energy outputs that have been measured outside the body, there are other subtle forces acting within the body that are not yet understood by science. The Soviet researcher, Dr. Alexandre Dubrow, has found that during mitosis or the splitting of cells, there's photon radiation from the cells. As you know, photons are particle waves of light, this radiation produces a dim glow, which we might call bioluminescence. The photon emissions produced by the cells in our bodies are in the ultraviolet frequencies beyond what we know as the visible spectrum.

All the trillions of cells in our bodies are emitting such photons from one to another. This emission does not stop at the skin surface, for the skin is also made up of cells. Perhaps this discovery helps us to understand some of the ancient references to light in the sacred texts. The Christian scriptures say you are light, and if therefore then I am single, their whole body shall be full of light. The meaning of that fascinating statement may not be purely symbolic or philosophical in Egyptian religion. A related image, the so-called Eye Horus, has been looked upon as the eye symbolizing health. Well, what is meant by the single eye, as long as we see positive and negative as two separate things.

There is no light. If you have a positive energy field and a negative energy field and they do not merge, there's no current. So if you still see something out of your right eye that is different from what you see with your left eye, there is an unbalanced condition. You are not perceiving things in their wholeness. So you are not in a healthy state. We know that in the human body, fluids are suspended in crystals as colloidal, those cells or crystalline substances. In another series of Soviet experiments replicated thousands of times, researchers put single cells in each of two glass test tubes. They first measured the electronic potential of each cell and its biochemical composition. The two test tubes were then placed next to each other and nothing happened.

The experimenter is next injected into one of the test tubes, substances that would disturb the physiological state of the single cell so that it would become different electronically and biochemically from the other, making it, in effect, a disease cell. As long as the cells were in the glass test tubes, nothing happened. The seesaw continued to be dismissed and the healthy cell continued to be healthy. The scientists then caught it between the cells, actually, they put the cells in test tubes. Immediately, they reported there was what they call a mirror image effect. Within seconds, the healthy cells started to show symptoms similar to those of the disease cells.

Do and his colleagues were able to measure at that time ultraviolet photo transference from one cell to the other. We know then that the crystalline part of our cellular structure is emitting photons in the ultraviolet wavelengths. You researchers have observed that during mitosis, the cell emits not only light, but also very high frequency sound. They found that it is possible to measure such ultrasonic sound within the body wherever there is light. Then there is also sound. Of course, such sound goes beyond the frequencies that we can hear. Eventually, we will be able to hear the sounds of our body by amplifying and translating them so that they become perceptible to our senses.

And we may then be able to diagnose those signals as one means of detecting illness. Knowledge that was once thought, as is now becoming exothermic, is becoming scientific knowledge. I believe that within the next five or 10 years, you may well be able to step into an instrument, be surrounded by an electrostatic field and immediately see a display on screens of what is happening in your body, in living colors, and you will see or hear the sound of your own body. If this can be amplified and made visible and audible to us, diagnostics will become much easier because as we shall see later on, it is possible to tell a great deal about the state of a person's health from the patterns of ammunition and absorption in his or her energy fields. Educating the senses.

If we realize that the human body is surrounded by energy fuels that can be detected by sensitive instruments like the squid, we will have a better understanding of what is meant by the aura. For many people, the aura has acquired a metaphysical meaning, and it was often felt that the aura is not really there or that it can be seen only by very highly developed, sensitive spiritual beings. This is a fallacy. What prevents you from seeing the aura is the fact that your eyesight is not properly educated. If you start educating your eyes, which you will learn to do in Chapter four, you will have a greater ability to perceive the activity taking place in so-called material objects. I've seen people who are absolutely non-spiritual, develop their physical vision properly and learn to see energy fields around others.

I must emphasize that with proper Chapter of your eyesight, you can observe energy fields emanating not only from the human body, but also from all material substances, including plants and inanimate matter. It is not an insult to the species to say that a plant or a rock can have an energy field. The human body is made up of exactly the same materials as animals, vegetables and minerals. All the elements in our bodies are the same as elements that can be found in the crust and the atmosphere of the Earth. The only difference is that we have a higher level of activity within our bodies that gives us a higher energy input and output and therefore we have a higher level of consciousness.

When you expand your energy, you automatically go beyond the or state and things become subtler, clearer and easier to perceive with the senses. We might make an analogy between two substances such as water and molasses. Both are fluid, but the molasses is thick, dense and practically opaque, whereas water is free and clear and flowing. The same thing is true of the human body in relation to the rest of the world. We seem to be more flexible, more expendable, and therefore we have a capacity for higher consciousness. We are able to radiate more and further and we are correspondingly more sensitive to things further beyond our own means. Some authentic riders proclaim that in order to pursue what we call God the universal, the environment beyond the human environment, one has to have an extra sense.

We have enough trouble with the five senses we've got, so let's not make it more difficult by adding another one to the list, you do not have to be psychic as every book on earth seems to tell you, in order to see the energy fields around human beings. So get away from the idea that you have to be a special person to do it. We are living in a three dimensional world and beyond our three dimensional world, there exists a multi dimensional world which we call the universe. When we speak of certain energy fields as we have measured them on planet Earth, we have to realize that is only how we have perceived them in the human environment, in Earth's environment and in our own solar system. Beyond that, we really do not know in what form the energy occurs. Some people often actually receive something from those planes beyond the human environment, our planet's environment, our solar system and even our galaxy.

This experience is multidimensional and it is impossible to recount such experiences in three dimensional language. But do not get the mistaken idea that you do not use your five senses for such perception, your five senses are the receptors for any visual, auditory, tactile, olfactory and gustatory images that you perceive. No matter what form such images may represent on a multidimensional plane, once these images have been perceived by the senses of the physical body, they are translated into physiological events in this three dimensional world. Although we are limited to our five senses, they can be greatly expanded and made much more sensitive. We're capable of becoming hyper static or hypersensitive through our five senses.

The state expands our capacity to tune in and enables us to go beyond our own immediate environment. Note the similarity between in tune with an intuitive. This is not a mysterious state beyond our understanding, it can be translated into the physical because we use our physical bodies and our senses for it. Such hyper static states can be evoked by hypnotic suggestion under normal circumstances, a person might not be able to perceive a certain stimulus with his or her senses. But through hypnosis, it is possible to increase the sensitivity of his or her perception to a higher level. In one experiment, for example, a subject could read a book held five feet in front of him, but if it was held at a much greater distance away, he could no longer read it.

The subject was then hypnotized and given special opaque glasses that had mirrors on the insides of the glass so that he could look in the mirrors and see what was happening behind him. The book was then held 20 feet behind them and he could read it under hypnosis. His visual acuity had been heightened beyond the normal range of perception, his senses had been brought to the hydrostatic state. We're not finding that if a person has the proper motivation, the same sorts of feats can be performed without hypnosis. Such expanded sense perception, then, is physically. It is not information that is obtained physically. Originally, the Greek word psyche meant so later it came to mean mind, because since we really do not know what soul is, it was easier to refer to mind.

So we started referring to everything mental as part of the psyche. But the broader definition of psyche as soul is actually more accurate. We say all of my body is in my mind, but not all of my mind is in my body. The body is like an egg yolk floating in the cosmic egg white, which contains our individual minds and the cosmos itself is this shell. That is, the mind or psyche operates as much outside as inside the body as distinguished from mine, the brain is the body's computer which perceives, directs and activates all the different transistors, tubes. And why is that? We call our physiological organs and you look at miracles. I recently made a trip to Europe specifically to investigate stories about some of the Christian saints.

One of the things you're particularly fascinated me was the medieval Saint Nicholas of you, who was a great historical figure from Switzerland and thanks to whom the country was able to retain its neutral status and not get involved in wars. I visited the area where Nicholas had lived and talked with the pastor of the local church. The stories about, say, Nicholas, were familiar historical facts. This necklace was married and had 10 children, so we can hardly say he lived a static life. But after a certain time, with the consent of his wife, he left his family and went into the woods where he lived for some years. There he began to eat less and less food until finally he stopped eating and drinking altogether. You lived on for 19 and a half years after that with no intake of food.

Of course, the statement is not quite accurate because the body cannot survive without nourishment, but as we shall see later, it was a different kind of nourishment that sustains St. Nicholas. When I visited Assisi in Italy on the same trip,

I was very fortunate to be allowed to visit the rooms that served as a virtual prison for Joseph of Cupertino, who is called the Flying Friar. Hanging in these rooms, there are pictures which have never been seen by the public showing St. Joseph levitating. It was because he did such strange things at strange times that the authorities tried to hide him, he was kept locked up in his rooms underneath the church in Assisi. He lived there for years and ate and drank hardly anything, but he levitated all the time.

All church documents tell the story of how one day a huge iron cross had to be put on top of the steeple of the church, and several men were trying to get this cross up but could not do it. St. Joseph was sent for. He looked at the cross and said, oh, that's nothing. Grab the cross, levitated with it and put it on top of the steeple all by himself. I heard stories about Joseph of Cupertino from a Franciscan friar who told me that documentation of these things had been unearthed from the Vatican archives.

Through this first account, I gained much better insight into the stories of the site that removed them from the realm of myth and superstition. Interestingly, St. Joseph of Cupertino did not have a crucifix or an image of the baby Jesus where he said his players said he had a statue of Mary as a baby. He was obviously very much aware of the feminine intuitive capacities, and he took the baby, Mary, as his inspiration.

Chapter - 3

Measured the electronic potential of each cell and its biochemical composition. The two test tubes were then placed next to each other and nothing happened. The experimenter is next injected into one of the test tubes, substances that would disturb the physiological state of the single cell so that it would become different electronically and biochemically from the other, making it, in effect, a disease cell. As long as the cells were in the glass test tubes, nothing happened. The sea continued to be seized and the healthy cell continued to be healthy. The scientists then caught a few between the cells, actually, they put the cells in test tubes. Immediately, they reported there was what they call a mirror image effect.

Within seconds, the healthy cells started to show symptoms similar to those of the disease cells. Do and his colleagues were able to measure at that time ultraviolet photo transference from one cell to the other. We know then that the crystalline part of our cellular structure is emitting photons in the ultraviolet wavelengths. Do researchers have observed that during mitosis, the cell emits not only light, but also very high frequency sound? They found that it is possible to measure such ultrasonic sound within the body wherever there is light. Then there is also sound. Of course, such sound goes beyond the frequencies that we can hear.

Eventually, we will be able to hear the sounds of our body by amplifying and translating them so that they become perceptible to our senses. And we may then be able to diagnose those signals as one means of detecting illness. Knowledge that was once thought esoteric is now becoming exothermic, it is becoming scientific knowledge. I believe that within the next five or 10 years, you may well be able to step into an instrument, be surrounded by an electrostatic field and immediately see a display on screens of what is happening in your body, in living colors, and you will see or hear the sound of your own body. If this can be amplified and made visible and audible to us, diagnostics will become much easier because as we shall see later on, it is possible to tell a great deal about the state of a person's health from the patterns of ammunition and absorption in his or her energy fields. Educating the senses.

If we realize that the human body is surrounded by energy fields that can be detected by sensitive instruments like the squid, we will have a better understanding of what is meant by the aura. For many people, the aura has acquired a metaphysical meaning, and it was often felt that the aura is not really there or that it can be seen only by very highly developed, sensitive spiritual beings. This is a fallacy. What prevents you from seeing the aura is the fact that your eyesight is not properly educated. If you start educating your eyes, which you will learn to do in Chapter four, you will have a greater ability to perceive the activity taking place in so-called material objects. I've seen people who are absolutely non-spiritual, develop their physical vision properly and learn to see energy fields around others.

I must emphasize that with proper Chapter of your eyesight, you can observe energy fields emanating not only from the human body, but also from all material substances, including plants and inanimate matter. It is not an insult to the higher species to say that a plant or a rock can have an energy field. The human body is made up of exactly the same materials as animals, vegetables and minerals. All the elements in our bodies are the same as elements that can be found in the crust and the atmosphere of the Earth. The only difference is that we have a higher level of activity within our bodies that gives us a higher energy input and output and therefore we have a higher level of consciousness.

When you expand your energy, you automatically go beyond the denser state and things become subtler, clearer and easier to perceive with the senses. We might make an analogy between two substances such as water and molasses. Both are fluid, but the molasses is thick, dense and practically opaque, whereas water is free and clear and flowing. The same thing is true of the human body in relation to the rest of the world. We seem to be more flexible, more expendable, and therefore we have a capacity for higher consciousness. We are able to radiate more and further and we are correspondingly more sensitive to things further beyond our own means.

Some esoteric writers proclaim that in order to pursue what we call God the universal, the environment beyond the human environment, one has to have an extra sense. We have enough trouble with the five senses we've got, so let's not make it more difficult by adding another one to the list, you do not have to be psychic as every book on Earth seems to tell you in order to see the energy fields around human beings. So get away from the idea that you have to be a special person to do it. We are living in a three dimensional world and beyond our three dimensional world, there exists a multidimensional world which we call the universe.

When we speak of certain energy fields as we have measured them on planet Earth, we have to realize that is only how we have perceived them in the human environment, in Earth's environment and in our own solar system. Beyond that, we really do not know in what form the energy occurs. Some people often actually receive something from those planes beyond the human environment, our planet's environment, our solar system and even our galaxy. This experience is multidimensional and it is impossible to recount such experiences in three dimensional language. But do not get the mistaken idea that you do not use your five senses for such perception, your five senses are the receptors for any visual, auditory, tactile, olfactory and gustatory images that you perceive.

No matter what form such images may represent on a multidimensional plane, once these images have been perceived by the senses of the physical body, they're translated into physiological events in this three dimensional world. Although we are limited to our five senses, they can be greatly expanded and made much more sensitive. We're capable of becoming hyper static or hypersensitive through our five senses. The state expands our capacity to tune in and enables us to go beyond our own immediate environment.

Note the similarity between in tune with and intuitive, this is not a mysterious state beyond our understanding, it can be translated into the physical because we use our physical bodies and our senses for it. Such hyper static states can be evoked by hypnotic suggestion under normal circumstances, a person might not be able to perceive a certain stimulus with his or her senses. But through hypnosis, it is possible to increase the sensitivity of his or her perception to a higher level. In one experiment, for example, a subject could read a book held five feet in front of him, but if it was held at a much greater distance away, he could no longer read it. The subject was then hypnotized and given special opaque glasses that had mirrors on the insides of the glass so that he could look in the mirrors and see what was happening behind him.

The book was then held 20 feet behind them and he could read it under hypnosis. His visual acuity had been heightened beyond the normal range of perception, his senses had been brought to the hyper aesthetic state. We're not finding that if a person has the proper motivation, the same sorts of feats can be performed without hypnosis. Such expanded sense perception, then, is physically. It is not information that is obtained physically. Originally, the Greek word psyche meant so later it came to me in mind because since we really do not know what soul is, it was easier to refer to mind. So we started referring to everything mental as part of the psyche. But the broader definition of psyche as soul is actually more accurate.

We say all of my body is in my mind, but not all of my mind is in my body. The body is like an egg yolk floating in the cosmic egg white, which contains our individual minds and the cosmos itself is this shell. That is, the mind or psyche operates as much outside as inside the body as distinguished from mine, the brain is the body's computer which perceives, directs and activates all the different transistors, tubes. And why is that? We call our physiological organs and you look at miracles. I recently made a trip to Europe specifically to investigate stories about some of the Christian saints.

One of the things you're particularly fascinated me was the medieval Saint Nicholas of you with a great historical figure from Switzerland and thanks to whom the country was able to retain its neutral status and not get involved in wars. I visited the area where Nicholas had lived and talked with the pastor of the local church. To the people there, the stories about St. Nicholas were familiar historical facts. This Nicholas was married and had 10 children, so we can hardly say he lived a static life. But after a certain time, with the consent of his wife, he left his family and went into the woods where he lived for some years. There he began to eat less and less food until finally he stopped eating and drinking altogether.

You lived on for 19 and a half years after that with no intake of food. Of course, the statement is not quite accurate because the body cannot survive without nourishment, but as we shall see later, it was a different kind of nourishment that sustains St. Nicholas. When I visited Assisi in Italy on the same trip, I was very fortunate to be allowed to visit the rooms that served as a virtual prison for Joseph of Cupertino, who is called the Flying Friar. Hanging in these rooms, there are pictures which have never been seen by the public showing St. Joseph levitating. It was because he did such strange things at strange times that the authorities tried to hide him.

He was kept locked up in his rooms underneath the church in Assisi. He lived there for years and ate and drank hardly anything, but he levitated all the time. All church documents tell the story of how one day a huge iron cross had to be put on top of the steeple of the church, and several men were trying to get this cross up but could not do it. St. Joseph was sent for. He looked at the cross and said, oh, that's nothing. Grab the cross, levitated with it and put it on top of the steeple all by himself. I heard stories about Joseph of Cupertino from a Franciscan friar who told me that documentation of these things had been unearthed from the Vatican archives. Through this first account, I gained much better insight into the stories of the site that removed them from the realm of myth and superstition. Interestingly, St.

Joseph of Cupertino did not have a crucifix or an image of the baby Jesus where he said his players instead he had a statue of Mary as a baby. He was obviously very much aware of the feminine intuitive capacities, and he took the baby, Mary, as his inspiration. Although St. Joseph may have overdone it a little bit, he was not the only saint who was able to levitate. Actually all of us levitate, although we do not necessarily recognize it as such, because we think that in levitation, the actual physical body should leave the ground. Let us say you get up in the morning feeling depressed and grouchy, your energy is like a little packet of blood.

If you weigh one hundred and fifty pounds, you have a gravitational pull of one hundred and fifty pounds, all centered in one place, and you make indentations in the ground. But when you get up in the morning feeling excited about a project you're going to work on or about the people you're going to be with, you float through the house like a butterfly. What has happened? Your energy has expanded over a much greater area. It fills the whole room now. So your gravitational pull is distributed over a much greater area. And in reality, you're levitating. In the U.S., I also heard a great deal, of course, about St.

Francis. I was particularly interested to hear about the Japanese who would come to ask if these Japanese were non Catholics, perhaps Buddhist or Shinto. They knew none of the Christian mythology surrounding the renowned saint. These people were merely tourists. But when they heard the stories about St. Francis of Assisi and how he communicated with the animals and the plants, they would immediately understand the significance of these stories because through their own religious traditions, they would become very involved with the meditative process and would get in touch with the feelings associated with the stories of the saint. It is obvious that the miracles of the Catholic saints have very little to do with Catalyst's Per Say.

Rather, they show what happens when we get in tune with the energies of our environment, not just the physical environment, but all the levels of energy that surround this. Our own personal belief systems often get in the way of true knowledge, just as the imagery of Catholicism may enhance or impede our acceptance of the stories of the Saints, depending on what our own belief systems are. What are we to make of these stories of people who can live for years and years without eating and drinking? I know from personal experience that it is possible to live with very little food for thirty three years.

I lived on three meals a week and sometimes have been able to sustain my body for weeks with no food at all without consciously or intentionally being on a fast. The recent movement was under medical supervision, as well as under observation by the Catholic Church for some thirty five years. On Fridays, she would eat a little holy war for when she took communion, and that was reportedly the only food she took in during all those decades. I know such things are possible because they have been done by a number of individuals, including myself. What is really going on when people are able to live without food? In what follows, I will share with you some of my own ideas about this phenomenon.

Life as a nutrient. I'm eating all the time, even when I'm not taking in food, although not in the same way that one would usually call eating. I had the chance sometime ago to talk with John Art, the author of the book Health and Light. He was the man who was originally contracted by Walt Disney to make Time-lapse photographs of plants. You would begin, for example, with the butt of a fruit tree and film it for a full year to show its development from the bud into a flower, from the flower into fruit, until the fruit was completely ripe. He told me that when he did this with an apple, he was very successful, but then he tried doing it with the same lighting, with a pomegranate

Chapter - 4

As animals, vegetables and minerals. All the elements in our bodies are the same as elements that can be found in the crust and the atmosphere of the Earth. The only difference is that we have a higher level of activity within our bodies that gives us a higher energy input and output and therefore we have a higher level of consciousness. When you expand your energy, you automatically go beyond the denser state and things become subtler, clearer and easier to perceive with the senses. We might make an analogy between two substances such as water and molasses. Both are fluid, but the molasses is thick, dense and practically opaque, whereas water is free and clear and flowing.

The same thing is true of the human body in relation to the rest of the world. We seem to be more flexible, more expendable, and therefore we have a capacity for higher consciousness. We are able to radiate more and further and we are correspondingly more sensitive to things further beyond our own means. Some esoteric writers proclaim that in order to pursue what we call God the universal, the environment beyond the human environment, one has to have an extra sense. We have enough trouble with the five senses we've got, so let's not make it more difficult by adding another one to the list, you do not have to be psychic as every book on earth seems to tell you, in order to see the energy fields around human beings.

So get away from the idea that you have to be a special person to do it. We are living in a three dimensional world and beyond our three dimensional world, there exists a multi dimensional world which we call the universe. When we speak of certain energy fields as we have measured them on planet Earth, we have to realize that is only how we have perceived them in the human environment, in Earth's environment and in our own solar system. Beyond that, we really do not know in what form the energy occurs. Some people often actually receive something from those planes beyond the human environment, our planet's environment, our solar system and even our galaxy.

This experience is multidimensional and it is impossible to recount such experiences in three dimensional language. But do not get the mistaken idea that you do not use your five senses for such perception, your five senses are the receptors for any visual, auditory, tactile, olfactory and gustatory images that you perceive. No matter what form such images may represent on a multidimensional plane, once these images have been perceived by the senses of the physical body, they're translated into physiological events in this three dimensional world. Although we are limited to our five senses, they can be greatly expanded and made much more sensitive.

We're capable of becoming hydrostatic or hypersensitive through our five senses. The hypersonics state expands our capacity to tune in and enables us to go beyond our own immediate environment. Note the similarity between in tune with and intuitive, this is not a mysterious state beyond our understanding, it can be translated into the physical because we use our physical bodies and our senses for it. Such hyper static states can be evoked by hypnotic suggestion under normal circumstances, a person might not be able to perceive a certain stimulus with his or her senses. But through hypnosis, it is possible to increase the sensitivity of his or her perception to a higher level.

In one experiment, for example, a subject could read a book held five feet in front of him, but if it was held at a much greater distance away, he could no longer read it. The subject was then hypnotized and given special opaque glasses that had mirrors on the insides of the glass so that he could look in the mirrors and see what was happening behind him. The book was then held 20 feet behind them and he could read it under hypnosis. His visual acuity had been heightened beyond the normal range of perception, his senses had been brought to the hyper aesthetic state. We're not finding that if a person has the proper motivation, the same sorts of feats can be performed without hypnosis.

Such expanded sense perception, then, is physically. It is not information that is obtained physically. Originally, the Greek word psyche meant soul, later it came to mind because since we really do not know what soul is, it was easier to refer to mind. So we started referring to everything mental as part of the psyche. But the broader definition of psyche as soul is actually more accurate. We say all of my body is in my mind, but not all of my mind is in my body. The body is like an egg yolk floating in the cosmic egg white, which contains our individual minds and the cosmos itself is this shell. That is, the mind or psyche operates as much outside as inside the body as distinguished from mine, the brain is the body's computer which perceives, directs and activates all the different transistors, tubes.

And why is that? We call our physiological organs and you look at miracles. I recently made a trip to Europe specifically to investigate stories about some of the Christian saints. One of the things you're particularly fascinated me was the medieval Saint Nicholas of you with a great historical figure from Switzerland and thanks to whom the country was able to retain its neutral status and not get involved in wars. I visited the area where Nicholas had lived and talked with the pastor of the local church. To the people there, the stories about St. Nicholas were familiar historical facts. This necklace was married and had 10 children, so we can hardly say he lived a static life.

But after a certain time, with the consent of his wife, he left his family and went into the woods where he lived for some years. There he began to eat less and less food until finally he stopped eating and drinking altogether. You lived on for 19 and a half years after that with no intake of food. Of course, the statement is not quite accurate because the body cannot survive without nourishment, but as we shall see later, it was a different kind of nourishment that sustains St. Nicholas. When I visited Assisi in Italy on the same trip, I was very fortunate to be allowed to visit the rooms that served as a virtual prison for Joseph of Cupertino, who is called the Flying Friar. Hanging in these rooms, there are pictures which have never been seen by the public showing St.

Joseph levitating. It was because he did such strange things at strange times that the authorities tried to hide him. He was kept locked up in his rooms underneath the church in Assisi. He lived there for years and ate and drank hardly anything, but he levitated all the time. All church documents tell the story of how one day a huge iron cross had to be put on top of the steeple of the church, and several men were trying to get this cross up but could not do it. St. Joseph was sent for. He looked at the cross and said, oh, that's nothing. Grab the cross, levitated with it and put it on top of the steeple all by himself.

I heard stories about Joseph of Cupertino from a Franciscan friar who told me that documentation of these things had been unearthed from the Vatican archives. Through this father's account, I gained much better insight into the stories of the state that removed them from the realm of myth and superstition. Interestingly, St. Joseph of Cupertino did not have a crucifix or an image of the baby Jesus where he said his players. Instead, he had a statue of Mary as a baby. He was obviously very much aware of the feminine intuitive capacities. And he took the baby, Mary, as his inspiration. Although St.

Joseph may have overdone it a little bit, he was not the only saint who was able to levitate. Actually all of us levitate, although we do not necessarily recognize it as such, because we think that in levitation, the actual physical body should leave the ground. What is that? You get up in the morning feeling depressed and grouchy, your energy is like a little packet of blood. If you weigh one hundred and fifty pounds, you have a gravitational pull of one hundred and fifty pounds, all centered in one place, and you make indentations in the ground. But when you get up in the morning feeling excited about a project you're going to work on or about the people you're going to be with, you float through the house like a butterfly. What has happened? Your energy has expanded over a much greater area.

It fills the whole room now. So your gravitational pull is distributed over a much greater area. And in reality, you're levitating. In the U.S., I also heard a great deal, of course, about St. Francis. I was particularly interested to hear about the Japanese who would come to ask if these Japanese were non Catholics, perhaps Buddhist or Shinto. They knew none of the Christian mythology surrounding the renowned saint. These people were merely tourists. But when they heard the stories about St. Francis of Assisi and how he communicated with the animals and the plants, they would immediately understand the significance of these stories because through their own religious traditions, they would become very involved with the meditative process and would get in touch with the feelings associated with the stories of the saint. It is obvious that the miracles of the Catholic saints have very little to do with Catalyst's the.

Rather, they show what happens when we get in tune with the energies of our environment, not just the physical environment, but all the levels of energy that surround this.

Our own personal belief systems often get in the way of true knowledge, just as the imagery of Catholicism may enhance or impede our acceptance of the stories of the Saints, depending on what our own belief systems are. What are we to make of these stories of people who can live for years and years without eating and drinking? I know from personal experience that it is possible to live with very little food for thirty three years. I lived on three meals a week and sometimes have been able to sustain my body for weeks with no food at all without consciously or intentionally being on a fast.

The recent movement was under medical supervision, as well as under observation by the Catholic Church for some thirty five years on Fridays, she would eat a little holy war for when she took communion. And that was reportedly the only food she took in during all those decades. I know such things are possible because they have been done by a number of individuals, including myself. What is really going on when people are able to live without food? In what follows, I will share with you some of my own ideas about this phenomenon. Life as a nutrient. I'm eating all the time, even when I'm not taking in food, although not in the same way that one would usually call eating.

I had the chance sometime ago to talk with John Ott, the author of the book Health and Light. He was the man who was originally contracted by Walt Disney to make Time-lapse photographs of plants. You would begin, for example, with the butt of a fruit tree and film it for a full year to show its development from the bud into a flower, from the flower into fruit, until the fruit was completely ripe. He told me that when he did this with an apple, he was very successful, but then he tried doing it with the same lighting, with a pomegranate, and it did not work. His whole year's work was ruined because he was filming with the same light and the pomegranate just did not want to grow. He then began to notice the effect of light on human bodies, as well as on the animals who were also in that environment.

He has set up the Institute of Research in Florida and is discovering the amazing influence that it has on us. Sources tell us that the Pentagon takes in life and even that some reptiles see only by their Pentagon, not by their eyes at all. John Orte shares with me the idea that we human beings are very similar to plants in certain respects. Plants use the light from the sun, which interact with their chlorophyll to manufacture their own food. We are higher up on the food chain, but all the nutrients, we can ultimately be traced to the plant and to the energy that comes from the sun. Now, why should we have to go through all these middlemen when we can get our energy directly from the wholesaler, if we human beings like plants use it as a nutrient and a source of energy? This is not to say, of course, that we photosynthesise like plants.

How can it be possible for us to live on light in energy fields when we go beyond the atomic level, we get to the electromagnetic level. Beyond that is the paradigmatic, which is different from Earth magnetism, where we see that positive attracts negative. That is that opposites attract. Brother empower magnetic fields like attracts like, so that if we radiate out a certain frequency of energy with a certain amplitude, this will attract energy of the same frequency and amplitude. If we are radiating energy from our bodies, we thereby attract from the environment an equal particle of the same frequency and the same amplitude. We've already seen not only that, there's intuitive psychic evidence that the human being radiates photons, but also that such radiation has been observed experimentally.

The brightness of this light or photon radiation is determined by the amplitude of the radiation, the higher the degree of excitement, the higher the amplitude and the brighter the ammunition. Our consciousness is not aware of our relationship to all these particles we attract from our environment, but once we understand the principles involved, it is not so strange that we could feed ourselves in that manner. It is very distressing to think that we in the western world, particularly in the United States, who have five percent of the total population of the world, have taken 50 percent of the Earth's resources and that this is still the most malnourished country in the world.

Because of our materialistic ideas, we have not been able to take from the environment those ingredients that can help us survive and be free of disease. The high energy output that surrounds the human being is not only a means by which we nourish ourselves by attracting other energy of the same frequency and amplitude. It is also a means of protecting ourselves because nothing from a lower energy field can enter a higher energy field because the higher energy will disintegrate, the lower. However, we must be careful not to deceive ourselves when we think of this ammunition as a means of protection. I have often heard people say I put light around me every day.

Chapter - 5

Greater distance away, he could no longer be. The subject was then hypnotized and given special opaque glasses that had mirrors on the insides of the glass, so that they could look in the mirrors and see what was happening behind them. The book was then held 20 feet behind them and he could read it under hypnosis. His visual acuity had been heightened beyond the normal range of perception, his senses had been brought to the hyper state. We're not finding that if a person has the proper motivation, the same sorts of feats can be performed without hypnosis. Such expanded sense perception, then, is physically. It is not information that is obtained physically. Originally, the Greek word psyche meant soul, so later it came to me in my mind because since we really do not know what soul is, it was easier to refer to mind.

So we started referring to everything mental as part of the psyche, but the broader definition of psyche, soul, is actually more accurate. We say all of my body is in my mind, but not all of my mind is in my body. The body is like an egg yolk floating in the cosmic egg white, which contains our individual minds and the cosmos itself is this shell. That is, the mind or psyche operates as much outside as inside the body as distinguished from mine, the brain is the body's computer which perceives, directs and activates all the different transistors, tubes. And why is that? We call our physiological organs and you look at miracles. I recently made a trip to Europe specifically to investigate stories about some of the Christian saints.

One of the things you're particularly fascinated me was the medieval Saint Nicholas of you, who was a great historical figure from Switzerland and thanks to whom the country was able to retain its neutral status and not get involved in wars. I visited the area where Nicholas had lived and talked with the pastor of the local church. To the people there, the stories about, say, Nicholas, were familiar historical facts. This necklace was married and had 10 children, so we can hardly say he lived a static life. But after a certain time, with the consent of his wife, he left his family and went into the woods where he lived for some years.

There he began to eat less and less food until finally he stopped eating and drinking altogether. You lived on for 19 and a half years after that with no intake of food. Of course, the statement is not quite accurate because the body cannot survive without nourishment, but as we shall see later, it was a different kind of nourishment that sustains St. Nicholas. When I visited Assisi in Italy on the same trip, I was very fortunate to be allowed to visit the rooms that served as a virtual prison for Joseph of Cupertino, who is called the Flying Friar.

Hanging in these rooms, there are pictures which have never been seen by the public showing St. Joseph levitating. It was because he did such strange things at strange times that the authorities tried to hide him. He was kept locked up in his rooms underneath the church in Assisi. He lived there for years and ate and drank hardly anything, but he levitated all the time. All church documents tell the story of how one day a huge iron cross had to be put on top of the steeple of the church, and several men were trying to get this cross up but could not do it. St. Joseph was sent for. He looked at the cross and said, oh, that's nothing. Grab the cross, levitated with it and put it on top of the steeple all by himself.

I heard stories about Joseph of Cupertino from a Franciscan friar who told me that documentation of these things had been unearthed from the Vatican archives. Through this first account, I gained much better insight into the stories of the state that removed them from the realm of myth and superstition. Interestingly, St. Joseph of Cupertino did not have a crucifix or an image of the baby Jesus where he said his players said he had a statue of Mary as a baby. He was obviously very much aware of the feminine intuitive capacities, and he took the baby, Mary, as his inspiration. Although St. Joseph may have overdone it a little bit, he was not the only saint who was able to levitate.

Actually all of us levitate, although we do not necessarily recognize it as such, because we think that in levitation, the actual physical body should leave the ground. Let us say you get up in the morning feeling depressed and grouchy, your energy is like a little packet of blood. If you weigh one hundred and fifty pounds, you have a gravitational pull of one hundred and fifty pounds, all centered in one place, and you make indentations in the ground. But when you get up in the morning feeling excited about a project you're going to work on or about the people you're going to be with, you float through the house like a butterfly. What has happened? Your energy has expanded over a much greater area.

It fills the whole room now. So your gravitational pull is distributed over a much greater area. And in reality, you're levitating. In Assisi, I also heard a great deal, of course, about St. Francis. I was particularly interested to hear about the Japanese who would come to ask if these Japanese were non Catholics, perhaps Buddhist or Shinto. They knew none of the Christian mythology surrounding the renowned saint, these people were merely tourists. But when they heard the stories about St. Francis of Assisi and how he communicated with the animals and the plants, they would immediately understand the significance of these stories because through their own religious traditions, they would become very involved with the meditative process and would get in touch with the feelings associated with the stories of the saint.

It is obvious that the miracles of the Catholic saints have very little to do with Catalyst's, per say. Rather, they show what happens when we get in tune with the energies of our environment, not just the physical environment, but all the levels of energy that surround this. Our own personal belief systems often get in the way of true knowledge, just as the imagery of Catholicism enhances or impedes our acceptance of the stories of the Saints, depending on what our own belief systems are. What are we to make of these stories of people who can live for years and years without eating and drinking? I know from personal experience that it is possible to live with very little food for thirty three years.

I lived on three meals a week and sometimes have been able to sustain my body for weeks with no food at all without consciously or intentionally being on a fast. The recent movement was under medical supervision, as well as under observation by the Catholic Church for some thirty five years. On Fridays, she would eat a little holy war for when she took communion, and that was reportedly the only food she took in during all those decades. I know such things are possible because they have been done by a number of individuals, including myself. What is really going on when people are able to live without food? In what follows, I will share with you some of my own ideas about this phenomenon.

Light as a nutrient. I'm eating all the time, even when I'm not taking in food, although not in the same way that one would usually call eating. I had the chance sometime ago to talk with John Art, the author of the book Health and Light. He was the man who was originally contracted by Walt Disney to make Time-lapse photographs of plants. You would begin, for example, with the butt of a fruit tree and film it for a full year to show its development from the bud into a flower, from the flower into fruit, until the fruit was complete. He told me that when he did this with an apple, he was very successful, but then he tried doing it with the same lighting, with a pomegranate, and it did not work.

His whole year's work was ruined because he was filming with the same light and the pomegranate just did not want to grow. He then began to notice the effect of light on human bodies, as well as on the animals who were also in that environment. He has set up the Institute of Research in Florida and is discovering the amazing influence that has on us. Sources tell us that the pineal gland takes sunlight and even that some reptiles see only by their blood, not by their eyes at all. John, AWT shares with me the idea that we human beings are very similar to plants in certain respects. Plants use the light from the sun, which interact with their chlorophyll to manufacture their own food.

We are higher up on the food chain, but all the nutrients, we can ultimately be traced to the plant and to the energy that comes from the sun. Now, why should we have to go through all these middlemen when we can get our energy directly from the wholesaler, if we human beings like plants use that as a nutrient and a source of energy? This is not to say, of course, that we photosynthesise like plants. How can it be possible for us to live on like? In energy fields, when we go beyond the atomic level, we get to the electromagnetic level. Beyond that is the paradigmatic, which is different from Earth magnetism, where we see that positive attracts negative, that is that opposites attract.

Brother and power magnetic fields attract like so that if we radiate out a certain frequency of energy with a certain amplitude, this will attract energy of the same frequency and amplitude. If we are radiating energy from our bodies, we thereby attract from the environment an equal particle of the same frequency and the same amplitude. We've already seen not only that, there's intuitive psychic evidence that the human being radiates photons, but also that such radiation has been observed experimentally. The brightness of this light or photon radiation is determined by the amplitude of the radiation, the higher the degree of excitement, the higher the amplitude and the brighter the ammunition.

Our consciousness is not aware of our relationship to all these particles we attract from our environment, but once we understand the principles involved, it is not so strange that we could feed ourselves in that manner. It is very distressing to think that we in the western world, particularly in the United States, who have five percent of the total population of the world, have taken 50 percent of the Earth's resources and that this is still the most malnourished country in the world. Because of our materialistic ideas, we have not been able to take from the environment those ingredients that can help us survive and be free of disease.

The high energy output that surrounds the human being is not only a means by which we nourish ourselves by attracting other energy of the same frequency and amplitude. It is also a means of protecting ourselves because nothing from a lower energy field can enter a higher energy field because the higher energy will disintegrate, the lower. However, we must be careful not to deceive ourselves when we think of this ammunition as a means of protection. I have often heard people say I put light around me every day that should protect me. But remember that creating an image in the conscious imagination is quite different from creating the energy itself and thereby producing that light.

Thinking let around you does not make light, in fact, when you think light, if you keep thinking and looking for that light, you're occupying your cerebral cortex. And when the cerebral cortex is occupied with the thinking process, it cannot create an outward flow of energy. Therefore, a lot of people who think a lot are constantly worried. Should I or shouldn't I? Or maybe, maybe not. That is, people who engage in the kinds of mental activity generally associated with better brain waves have been known to get tension headaches and migraines. They also have poor blood circulation because in order to think you have to have energy and in order to have energy in the brain, you need oxygen and glucose for fuel. And these have to be brought in by the blood, the trucking company.

So if you get all that thinking going, the blood is occupied with bringing whole truckloads of fuel to the brain. As a result, you do not get it to your hands, to your feet or through your body. And you have poor circulation, cold hands and cold feet. Perhaps it sounds a little far-fetched to say that too much attachment to thinking can cause such physical problems. However, clinical medical experience has borne out these observations. To overcome the symptomatic results of excessive cerebral blood flow, the Menninger Foundation, with special temperature biofeedback Chapter techniques, helps people learn to divert excessive blood flow from the cerebral area back to the peripheral or parts of the circulatory system, such as the hands and the feet.

This is actually nothing more than learning to make the head cool and the hands and feet warm to bring the blood away in the non-thinking process in the passive nonvolatile way. Such techniques are now being used successfully all over the country in the treatment of migraine and tension headaches. I am not saying that all thinking is bad. Thinking goes on in the unconscious as well as in the conscious mind, the unconscious mind has as much selectivity and discrimination as the conscious mind, and therefore a great deal of unconscious activity could also be called thinking.

The kind of thinking process that can lead to problems is one in which we attach ourselves to the problem, to the thought itself and thereby hold onto the problem rather than release the energy and the emotion associated with it. The brain needs nourishment for this kind of activity to hold the thought there, to imprison it, and the blood therefore flows to the cerebral area. What I call decisive thinking is quite the opposite. It is a release of energy as soon as one decides, one releases. Often we do not really look for solutions when we are involved in problem solving. We claim we do, but we actually attach ourselves to the problem. That is what causes the pressure in the head. The worry and the physiological disturbances. But when thinking leads to release, often through unconscious processes, the physiological vicious cycle does not have a chance to get started.

This should explain why consciously putting light around yourself might not necessarily be helpful to you at all. There are methods for putting this energy around you, and the best method is, of course, to have a normal regulated function of all the organs in your body, which means that all the chakras or subtle energy centers have to be operating at full capacity.

Let us now see how these truckers are involved in the energy output of the human organism. A practical review of the chakras. There is a great deal of misunderstanding about the choppers, about so many metaphysical systems, it is difficult to resolve the different modes of expression used to describe the chakra system. When I discuss the chakras, therefore, I am only sharing what I've observed in the thirty five years that I have been able to see the chakras and their energy fields and what they do in the body.

Chapter - 6

That documentation of these things had been unearthed from the Vatican archives. Through this father's account, I gained much better insight into the stories of the state that removed them from the realm of myth and superstition. Interestingly, St. Joseph of Cupertino did not have a crucifix or an image of the baby Jesus where he said his players. Instead, he had a statue of Mary as a baby. He was obviously very much aware of the feminine intuitive capacities. And he took the baby, Mary, as his inspiration. Although St. Joseph may have overdone it a little bit, he was not the only saint who was able to levitate. Actually all of us levitate, although we do not necessarily recognize it as such, because we think that in levitation, the actual physical body should leave the ground.

Let us say you get up in the morning feeling depressed and grouchy, your energy is like a little packet of blood. If you weigh one hundred and fifty pounds, you have a gravitational pull of one hundred and fifty pounds, all centered in one place, and you make indentations in the ground. But when you get up in the morning feeling excited about a project you're going to work on or about the people who are going to be with you float through the house like a butterfly, what has happened? Your energy has expanded over a much greater area. It fills the whole room now. So your gravitational pull is distributed over a much greater area and in reality, you're levitating. In Assisi, I also heard a great deal, of course, about St. Francis.

I was particularly interested to hear about the Japanese who would come to ask if these Japanese were non Catholics, perhaps Buddhist or Shinto. They knew none of the Christian mythology surrounding the renowned saint. These people were merely tourists. But when they heard the stories about St. Francis of Assisi and how he communicated with the animals and the plants, they would immediately understand the significance of these stories because through their own religious traditions, they would become very involved with the meditative process and would get in touch with the feelings associated with the stories of the saint. It is obvious that the miracles of the Catholic saints have very little to do with Catalyst's per say.

Rather, they show what happens when we get in tune with the energies of our environment, not just the physical environment, but all the levels of energy that surround this. Our own personal belief systems often get in the way of true knowledge, just as the imagery of Catholicism enhances or impedes our acceptance of the stories of the Saints, depending on what our own belief systems are. What are we to make of these stories of people who can live for years and years without eating and drinking? I know from personal experience that it is possible to live with very little food. For thirty three years, I lived on three meals a week and sometimes have been able to sustain my body for weeks with no food at all without consciously or intentionally being on a fast.

The recent movement was under medical supervision, as well as under observation by the Catholic Church for some thirty five years. On Fridays, she would eat a little holy war for when she took communion, and that was reportedly the only food she took in during all those decades. I know such things are possible because they have been done by a number of individuals, including myself. What is really going on when people are able to live without food? In what follows, I will share with you some of my own ideas about this phenomenon. Life as a nutrient. I'm eating all the time, even when I'm not taking in food, although not in the same way that one would usually call eating. I had the chance sometime ago to talk with John Art, the author of the book Health and Light.

He was the man who was originally contracted by Walt Disney to make Time-lapse photographs of plants. You would begin, for example, with the butt of a fruit tree and film it for a full year to show its development from the bud into a flower, from the flower into fruit, until the fruit was completely ripe. He told me that when he did this with an apple, he was very successful, but then he tried doing it with the same lighting, with a pomegranate, and it did not work. His whole year's work was ruined because he was filming with the same light and the pomegranate just did not want to grow. He then began to notice the effect of light on human bodies, as well as on the animals who were also in that environment.

He has since set up the Institute of Research in Florida and is discovering the amazing influence that has on us. Sources tell us that the Pentagon takes in life and even that some reptiles see only by their opinion, but not by their eyes at all. John Orte shares with me the idea that we human beings are very similar to plants in certain respects. Plants use the light from the sun, which interact with their chlorophyll to manufacture their own food. We are higher up on the food chain, but all the nutrients can ultimately be traced to plant life and to the energy that comes from the sun. Now, why should we have to go through all these middlemen when we can get our energy directly from the wholesaler, if we human beings like plants use it as a nutrient and a source of energy? This is not to say, of course, that we photosynthesise like plants.

How can it be possible for us to live on like? In energy fields, when we go beyond the atomic level, we get to the electromagnetic level. Beyond that is the paradigmatic, which is different from Earth magnetism, where we see that positive attracts negative, that is that opposites attract. Brother and paramedic feels like attracts like so that if we radiate out a certain frequency of energy with a certain amplitude, this will attract energy of the same frequency and amplitude. If we are radiating energy from our bodies, we thereby attract from the environment an equal particle of the same frequency and the same amplitude.

We've already seen not only that, there's intuitive psychic evidence that the human being radiates photons, but also that such radiation has been observed experimentally. The brightness of this light or photon radiation is determined by the amplitude of the radiation, the higher the degree of excitement, the higher the amplitude and the brighter the ammunition. Our consciousness is not aware of our relationship to all these particles we attract from our environment, but once we understand the principles involved, it is not so strange that we could feed ourselves in that manner. It is very distressing to think that we in the western world, particularly in the United States, who have five percent of the total population of the world, have taken 50 percent of the Earth's resources and that this is still the most malnourished country in the world.

Because of our materialistic ideas, we have not been able to take from the environment those ingredients that can help us survive and be free of disease. The high energy output that surrounds the human being is not only a means by which we nourish ourselves by attracting other energy of the same frequency and amplitude. It is also a means of protecting ourselves because nothing from a lower energy field can enter a higher energy field because the higher energy will disintegrate, the lower. However, we must be careful not to deceive ourselves when we think of this ammunition as a means of protection. I have often heard people say I put light around me every day that should protect me.

But remember that creating an image in the conscious imagination is quite different from creating the energy itself and thereby producing that light. Thinking let around you does not make light, in fact, when you think light, if you keep thinking and looking for that light, you're occupying your cerebral cortex. And when the cerebral cortex is occupied with the thinking process, it cannot create an outward flow of energy. Therefore, a lot of people who think a lot will constantly worry, should I or shouldn't I? Or maybe, maybe not. That is, people who engage in the kinds of mental activity generally associated with better brain waves have been known to get tension headaches and migraines. They also have poor blood circulation because in order to think you have to have energy and in order to have energy in the brain, you need oxygen and glucose for fuel. And these have to be brought in by the blood, the trucking company.

So if you get all that thinking going, the blood is occupied with bringing whole truckloads of fuel to the brain. As a result, you do not get it into your hands. To your feet or through your body, and you have poor circulation, cold hands and cold feet. Perhaps it sounds a little far-fetched to say that too much attachment to thinking can cause such physical problems. However, clinical medical experience has borne out these observations. To overcome the symptomatic results of excessive cerebral blood flow, the Menninger Foundation, with special temperature biofeedback Chapter techniques, helps people learn to divert excessive blood flow from the cerebral area back to the peripheral or parts of the circulatory system, such as the hands and the feet.

This is actually nothing more than learning to make the head cool and the hands and feet warm to bring the blood away in the non-thinking process in a passive nonvolatile way. Such techniques are now being used successfully all over the country in the treatment of migraine and tension headaches. I am not saying that all thinking is bad. Thinking goes on in the unconscious as well as in the conscious mind, the unconscious mind has as much selectivity and discrimination as the conscious mind, and therefore a great deal of unconscious activity could also be called thinking. The kind of thinking process that can lead to problems is one in which we attach ourselves to the problem, to the thought itself and thereby hold onto the problem rather than release the energy and the emotion associated with it.

The brain needs nourishment for this kind of activity to hold the thought there, to imprison it, and the blood therefore flows to the cerebral area. What I call decisive thinking is quite the opposite. It is a release of energy as soon as one decides, one releases. Often we do not really look for solutions when we are involved in problem solving, we claim we do, but we actually attach ourselves to the problem. That is what causes the pressure in the head. The worry and the physiological disturbances. But one thinking leads to release, often through unconscious processes, the physiological vicious cycle does not have a chance to get started. They should explain why consciously putting light around yourself might not necessarily be helpful to you at all.

There are methods for putting this energy around you, and the best method is, of course, to have a normal regulated function of all the organs in your body, which means that all the chakras or subtle energy centers have to be operating at full capacity. Let us now see how these choppers are involved in the energy output of the human organism. A practical review of the chakras. There is a great deal of misunderstanding about the choppers, about so many metaphysical systems, it is difficult to resolve the different modes of expression used to describe the chakra system.

When I discuss the chakras. Therefore, I am only sharing what I've observed in the thirty five years that I have been able to see the chakras and their energy field and what they do in the body. I am not really so interested in the philosophical aspects, rather, I prefer to focus on the practical applications of this knowledge.

I see too many people walking around absorbed in philosophy with their eyes on the sky, and it is obvious that they are deceased and they have all kinds of physiological problems. They are starry eyed, but have a slow body that makes very little sense to me if our knowledge cannot be practical, it has little value. This is not to deny the value of the spiritual side of life, but one cannot be spiritual without the proper direction of mind and without the proper physical vehicle through which the spirit can operate. According to people who can perceive these things, the body appears to have 13 subtle energy centers called chakras. Chocolate is the desperate word for word, the word was chosen because those who are able to observe the chakras by looking through the aura see them in cross Chapter as fast moving vortices of energy containing colors.

Six of the choppers are minor and their activities and seven are major, all seven major choppers except one interrelate with the endocrine system. Remember, however, that when I mention an endocrine gland connected with a particular chakra, I'm referring not to the chakra itself, but rather to the organ that is influenced by the energy field. The choppers should be thought of as Dynamo's dynamic centers through which the energy is distributed. This energy is distributed from the Choctaws as it comes into the body as well as when it goes out of the body.

Chapter - 7

During all those decades. I know such things are possible because they have been done by a number of individuals, including myself. What is really going on when people are able to live without food? In what follows, I will share with you some of my own ideas about this phenomenon. Light as a nutrient. I'm eating all the time, even when I'm not taking in food, although not in the same way that one would usually call eating. I had the chance sometime ago to talk with John Ott, the author of the book Health and Light. He was the man who was originally contracted by Walt Disney to make Time-lapse photographs of plants. You would begin, for example, with the butt of a fruit tree and film it for a full year to show its development from the bud into a flower, from the flower into fruit, until the fruit was completely ripe.

He told me that when he did this with an apple, he was very successful, but then he tried doing it with the same lighting, with a pomegranate, and it did not work. His whole year's work was ruined because he was filming with the same light and the pomegranate just did not want to grow. He then began to notice the effect of light on human bodies, as well as on the animals who were also in that environment. He has set up the Institute of Research in Florida and is discovering the amazing influence that it has on us. Sources tell us that the Pentagon takes in life and even that some reptiles see only by their Pentagon, not by their eyes at all.

John, AWT shares with me the idea that we human beings are very similar to plants in certain respects.

Plants use the light from the sun, which interact with their chlorophyll to manufacture their own food. We are higher up on the food chain for all the nutrients. We can ultimately be traced to the plant and to the energy that comes from the sun. Now, why should we have to go through all these middlemen when we can get our energy directly from the wholesaler, if we human beings like plants use it as a nutrient and a source of energy? This is not to say, of course, that we photosynthesise like plants. How can it be possible for us to live on like? In energy fields, when we go beyond the atomic level, we get to the electromagnetic level. Beyond that is the paradigmatic, which is different from Earth magnetism, where we see that positive attracts negative.

That is that opposites attract. Brother empower magnetic fields like attracts like. So that if we radiate out a certain frequency of energy with a certain amplitude, this will attract energy of the same frequency and amplitude. If we are radiating energy from our bodies, we thereby attract from the environment an equal particle of the same frequency and the same amplitude. We've already seen not only that, there's intuitive psychic evidence that the human being radiates photons, but also that such radiation has been observed experimentally. The brightness of this light or photon radiation is determined by the amplitude of the radiation, the higher the degree of excitement, the higher the amplitude and the brighter the ammunition.

Our consciousness is not aware of our relationship to all these particles we attract from our environment, but once we understand the principles involved, it is not so strange that we could feed ourselves in that manner. It is very distressing to think that we in the western world, particularly in the United States, who have five percent of the total population of the world, have taken 50 percent of the Earth's resources and that this is still the most malnourished country in the world. Because of our materialistic ideas, we have not been able to take from the environment those ingredients that can help us survive and be free of disease.

The high energy output that surrounds the human being is not only a means by which we nourish ourselves by attracting other energy of the same frequency and amplitude. It is also a means of protecting ourselves because nothing from a lower energy field can enter a higher energy field because the higher energy will disintegrate, the lower. However, we must be careful not to deceive ourselves when we think of this ammunition as a means of protection. I have often heard people say I put light around me every day that should protect me. But remember that creating an image in the conscious imagination is quite different from creating the energy itself and thereby producing that light.

Thinking let around you does not make light, in fact, when you think light, if you keep thinking and looking for that light, you're occupying your cerebral cortex. And when the cerebral cortex is occupied with the thinking process, it cannot create an outward flow of energy. Therefore, a lot of people who think a lot are constantly worried, should I or shouldn't I? Or maybe, maybe not. That is, people who engage in the kinds of mental activity generally associated with better brain waves have been known to get tension headaches and migraines. They also have poor blood circulation because in order to think you have to have energy and in order to have energy in the brain, you need oxygen and glucose for fuel. And these have to be brought in by the blood, the trucking company.

So if you get all that thinking going, the blood is occupied with bringing whole truckloads of fuel to the brain. As a result, you do not get it to your hands, to your feet or through your body. And you have poor circulation, cold hands and cold feet. Perhaps it sounds a little far-fetched to say that too much attachment to thinking can cause such physical problems. However, clinical medical experience has borne out these observations. To overcome the symptomatic results of excessive cerebral blood flow, the Menninger Foundation, with special temperature biofeedback Chapter techniques, helps people learn to divert excessive blood flow from the cerebral area back to the peripheral or parts of the circulatory system, such as the hands and the feet.

This is actually nothing more than learning to make the head cool and the hands and feet warm to bring the blood away in the non-thinking process in a passive nonvolatile way. Such techniques are now being used successfully all over the country in the treatment of migraine and tension headaches. I am not saying that all thinking is bad. Thinking goes on in the unconscious as well as in the conscious mind, the unconscious mind has as much selectivity and discrimination as the conscious mind, and therefore a great deal of unconscious activity could also be called thinking.

The kind of thinking process that can lead to problems is one in which we attach ourselves to the problem, to the thought itself and thereby hold onto the problem rather than release the energy and emotion associated with it. The brain needs nourishment for this kind of activity to hold the thought there, to imprison it, and the blood therefore flows to the cerebral area. What I call decisive thinking is quite the opposite. It is a release of energy as soon as one decides, one releases. Often we do not really look for solutions when we are involved in problem solving, we claim we do, but we actually attach ourselves to the problem. That is what causes the pressure in the head. The worry and the physiological disturbances.

But one thing leads to release, often through unconscious processes, the physiological vicious cycle does not have a chance to get started. They should explain why consciously putting light around yourself might not necessarily be helpful to you at all. There are methods for putting this energy around you, and the best method is, of course, to have a normal regulated function of all the organs in your body, which means that all the chakras or subtle energy centers have to be operating at full capacity. Let us now see how these choppers are involved in the energy output of the human organism.

A practical review of the chakras. There is a great deal of misunderstanding about the chakras, about so many metaphysical systems, it is difficult to resolve the different modes of expression used to describe the chakra system. When I discuss the chakras, therefore, I am only sharing what I've observed in the thirty five years that I have been able to see the chakras and their energy field and what they do in the body. I am not really so interested in the philosophical aspects, rather, I prefer to focus on the practical applications of this knowledge. I see too many people walking around absorbed in philosophy with their eyes on the sky, and it is obvious that they are deceased and they have all kinds of physiological problems.

They are starry eyed, but have a slow body that makes very little sense to me if our knowledge cannot be practical, it has little value. This is not to deny the value of the spiritual side of life, but one cannot be spiritual without the proper direction of mind and without the proper physical vehicle through which the spirit can operate. According to people who can perceive these things, the body appears to have 13 subtle energy centers called chakras. Chocolate is this desperate word for Wiel, the word was chosen because those who are able to observe the chakras by looking through the aura see them in cross Chapter as fast moving vortices of energy containing colors.

Six of the choppers are minor and their activities and seven are major, all seven major choppers except one interrelate with the endocrine system. Remember, however, that when I mention an endocrine gland connected with a particular chakra, I'm referring not to the chakra itself, but rather to the organ that is influenced by the energy field. The choppers should be thought of as Dynamo's dynamic centers through which the energy is distributed. This energy is distributed from the Choctaws as it comes into the body as well as when it goes out of the body. There is a capacity for transmission as well as for reception, the choppers are the centers that make the area brighter and brighter or dimmer and dimmer depending on their activity.

Each of the chakras vibrates at a characteristic frequency as it transmits energy, the energy pattern around each chakra is viewed as a vortex predominantly of a certain color, which corresponds to the frequency at which that chakras vibrate. Similarly, chakra is associated with a musical tone that also corresponds to the frequency of its basic vibration. When a chopper is operating in a balanced manner, the color surrounding it will be very pale and it will be the pure color of that chakra. The pale color indicates that the energy transmitted by the chakra is fine and subtle. If a chopper is not properly transmitting the energy that comes into it, the color will have a dense dark outflow that will be apparent in the aura surrounding the chopper.

In my earlier book, Voluntary Controls, I discussed at some length the characteristics of each of the chakras. In brief, each aircraft has an external physical counterpart in one of the seven major glands of the body. Each has a characteristic color and frequency of the vibration associated with the quality of the energy that's concerned with. Table table one characteristics of the chakras, chakra, root or sacral spinal location for the sacral vertebra, organ gonads. Color red or orange energy left promoting. Chakra spleen, spinal location, first, lumbar vertebra, organ, spleen. Color, pink, energy, reserve or love. Chakra, solar plexus, spinal location, a thoracic vertebra, organ, adrenals, color, green energy, life preserving. Chakra part. Spinal location, first, thoracic vertebra, organ blindness, color, gold, energy, mental or consciousness.

Chakra throat, spinal location, third cervical vertebrae, organ, thyroid color blue. Energy expressive. Jorquera, Brout, Spinel, location first, cervical vertebra, organ, pituitary color, indigo energy synthesizing. Chopra, Crout, spinal location, none, organ panel color. Palpable energy integration. The colors of the chakras are not in rainbow order. That is, the sequence of colors in the chakras from lowest to highest is not in the order of the spectrum. When we realize that each of the chakras resonates with a certain color, sound and frequency, it is easier to understand how color and sound can have a therapeutic effect.

They can help to stimulate and balance the activity of particular chakras. Involuntary controls, I outlined a series of Chopra exercises that enabled people to check the function of each chakra through meditation and color breathing. At the Veterans Hospital in Topeka, Kansas, psychotic patients were taught to do the choker exercises every day. Through these exercises, they were able to become calmer and their creativity was enhanced, so the Chalke exercises can be useful not only for monitoring our physiological functioning, but also to regulate our mental functioning. We know that there are physios, somatic diseases, but there are some metaphysic diseases as well. That is when your body does not operate properly.

Chapter - 8

Other energy of the same frequency and amplitude. It is also a means of protecting ourselves because nothing from a lower energy field can enter a higher energy field because the higher energy will disintegrate, the lower. However, we must be careful not to deceive ourselves when we think of this ammunition as a means of protection. I have often heard people say I put light around me every day that should protect me. But remember that creating an image in the conscious imagination is quite different from creating the energy itself and thereby producing that light. Thinking let around you does not make light. In fact, when you think light, if you keep thinking and looking for that light, you're occupying your cerebral cortex.

And when the cerebral cortex is occupied with the thinking process, it cannot create an outward flow of energy. Therefore, a lot of people who think a lot will constantly worry, should I or shouldn't I? Or maybe, maybe not. That is, people who engage in the kinds of mental activity generally associated with better brain waves have been known to get tension headaches and migraines. They also have poor blood circulation because in order to think you have to have energy and in order to have energy in the brain, you need oxygen and glucose for fuel. And these have to be brought in by the blood, the trucking company. So if you get all that thinking going, the blood is occupied with bringing whole truckloads of fuel to the brain.

As a result, you do not get it into your hands. Do your feet or throw your body and you have poor circulation, cold hands and cold feet. Perhaps it sounds a little far-fetched to say that too much attachment to thinking can cause such physical problems. However, clinical medical experience has borne out these observations. To overcome the symptomatic results of excessive cerebral blood flow, the Menninger Foundation, with special temperature biofeedback Chapter techniques, helps people learn to divert excessive blood flow from the cerebral area back to the peripheral or parts of the circulatory system, such as the hands and the feet. This is actually nothing more than learning to make the head cool and the hands and feet warm to bring the blood away in the non-thinking process in a passive nonvolatile way.

Such techniques are now being used successfully all over the country in the treatment of migraine and tension headaches. I am not saying that all thinking is bad. Thinking goes on in the unconscious as well as in the conscious mind, the unconscious mind has as much selectivity and discrimination as the conscious mind, and therefore a great deal of unconscious activity could also be called thinking. The kind of thinking process that can lead to problems is one in which we attach ourselves to the problem, to the thought itself and thereby hold onto the problem rather than release the energy and emotion associated with it. The brain needs nourishment for this kind of activity to hold the thought there, to imprison it, and the blood therefore flows to the cerebral area. What I call decisive thinking is quite the opposite.

It is a release of energy as soon as one decides, one releases. Often we do not really look for solutions when we are involved in problem solving. We claim we do, but we actually attach ourselves to the problem. That is what causes the pressure in the head. The worry and the physiological disturbances. But one thing leads to release, often through unconscious processes, the physiological vicious cycle does not have a chance to get started. They should explain why consciously putting light around yourself might not necessarily be helpful to you at all. There are methods for putting this energy around you, and the best method is, of course, to have a normal regulated function of all the organs in your body, which means that all the chakras or subtle energy centers have to be operating at full capacity.

Let us now see how these choppers are involved in the energy output of the human organism. A practical review of the chakras. There is a great deal of misunderstanding about the choppers, as with so many metaphysical systems, it is difficult to resolve the different modes of expression used to describe the chakra system. When I discuss the chakras, therefore I am only sharing what I've observed in the thirty five years that I have been able to see the chakras and their energy field and what they do in the body. I am not really so interested in the philosophical aspects, rather, I prefer to focus on the practical applications of this knowledge. I see too many people walking around absorbed in philosophy with their eyes on the sky, and it is obvious that they are deceased and they have all kinds of physiological problems.

They are starry eyed, but so body that makes very little sense to me if our knowledge cannot be practical. It has little value. This is not to deny the value of the spiritual side of life, but one cannot be spiritual without the proper direction of mind and without the proper physical vehicle through which the spirit can operate. According to people who can perceive these things, the body appears to have 13 subtle energy centers called chakras. Chakra is this desperate word for real, the word was chosen because those who are able to observe the chakras by looking through the aura see them in cross Chapter as fast moving vortices of energy containing colors. Six of the choppers are minor and their activities and seven are major, all seven major choppers except one interrelate with the endocrine system.

Remember, however, that when I mention an endocrine gland connected with a particular chakra, I'm referring not to the chakra itself, but rather to the organ that is influenced by the energy field. The choppers should be thought of as Dynamo's dynamic centers through which the energy is distributed. This energy is distributed from the Choctaws as it comes into the body as well as when it goes out of the body. There is a capacity for transmission as well as for reception, the choppers are the centers that make the area brighter and brighter or dimmer and dimmer depending on their activity. Each of the chakras vibrates at a characteristic frequency as it transmits energy, the energy pattern around each chakra is viewed as a vortex predominantly of a certain color, which corresponds to the frequency at which that chakras vibrate.

Similarly, each is associated with a musical tone that also corresponds to the frequency of its basic vibration. When a chopper is operating in a balanced manner, the culture surrounding it will be very pale and it will be the pure color of that chakra. The pale color indicates that the energy transmitted by the chakra is fine and subtle. If a chopper is not properly transmitting the energy that comes into it, the color will have a dense dark outflow that will be apparent in the aura surrounding the chakra. In my earlier book, Voluntary Controls, I discussed at some length the characteristics of each of the chakras. In brief, each aircraft has an external physical counterpart in one of the seven major glands of the body. Each has a characteristic color and frequency of the vibration associated with the quality of the energy that's concerned with.

Table one characteristics of the chakras, chakra, root or sacral spinal location for the sacral vertebral organ gonads. Color red or orange energy left promoting. Chakra spleen, spinal location, first, lumbar vertebra, organ, spleen. Color, pink, energy, reserve or love. Chakra, solar plexus, spinal location, a thoracic vertebra, organ, adrenals, color, green energy, life preserving. Chakra part. Spinal location, first, thoracic vertebra, organ thymus color, gold, energy, mental or consciousness. Chakra throat, spinal location, third cervical vertebrae, organ, thyroid color blue. Energy expressive. Jorquera, Brout, Spinel, location first, cervical vertebra, organ, pituitary color, indigo energy synthesizing. Chopra crown spinal location none, organ color, pale purple energy integration. The colors of the chakras are not in rainbow order.

That is, the sequence of colors in the chakras from lowest to highest is not in the order of the spectrum. When we realize that each of the chakras resonate with a certain color, sound and frequency, it is easier to understand how color and sound can have a therapeutic effect. They can help to stimulate imbalanced activity of particular chakras. Involuntary controls, I outlined a series of Chopra exercises that enabled people to check the function of each chakra through meditation and color breathing. At the Veterans Hospital in Topeka, Kansas, psychotic patients were taught to do the choker exercises every day. Through these exercises, they were able to become calmer and their creativity was enhanced, so the Chalke exercises can be useful not only for monitoring our physiological functioning, but also to regulate our mental functioning.

We know that there are physical somatic diseases, but there are some metaphysic diseases as well. That is when your body does not operate properly. You cannot do anything with it, no matter how powerful your mind is and how much you perceive it, if your mind does not have the instrument through which to express its perceptions. You are like the sculptor who has a fantastic image of a statue in his mind, but who does not have the clay or rock to chisel it out of the mental image, does not do anybody any good energy transformation through the chakras with their review of the function of the choppers in mind. Let us return to the question of how we can nourish ourselves on pure energy on white.

We shall see in Chapter two that just as there is an output of energy from the body, there's also an input which is called the ray. The bay takes the form of light and the color of the light that remains is the same for each individual throughout his lifetime. According to my personal observation, this light or current, which I've also called the rape, enters the body through the crown chakra, which is associated with the pineal gland. At this point, the energy is pure light, but as it moves down to the brow chakra, which is associated with the pituitary gland, it is broken down into seven different qualities. The pituitary functions as a prison and breaks down the light the same way a prison breaks what light into a spectrum, the pituitary refracts the lights and distributes throughout the body by way of the various chakras.

The pituitary is known as the master gland because of its role in regulating the function of the body through its hormonal secretions. As a subtle energy center, the pituitary or brow chakra plays a similar role in regulating and distributing energy. When the energy returns back up through the chuckers after it has been distributed to and utilized by the various organs and systems of the body, the brow or pituitary chakra functions as a synthesizer, integrating the component energies once again into pure white light. After the lid has been broken down into seven different qualities by the brow chakra, it moves down to the throat chakra, which is associated with the thyroid gland. Here is the first place where the light starts to become denser so that it can interact with the body chemistry and as it goes down through the subtle energy centers, it becomes progressively denser still.

A throat chakra, the seven qualities are divided into three groups, three qualities on the right, the male creative side, which deal with Anabel isn't the process of building up whereby new substances or chemistries or forms of substances are created. Three qualities on the left, the feminine, receptive side, which deal with metabolism, the process of breaking down substances, taking them out of the form in which they entered, and one quality in the middle, the catalyst which brings anapolis and capitalism together in the total process of metabolism. These qualities of energy are used to nourish the various systems of the body with each chakra drawing out the energy it requires.

I should make it clear that when I talk about energy transformations in this manner, I'm making a symbolic statement about what I actually observe. What I perceive as multidimensional planes of consciousness and energy fields, no matter how these things may occur objectively, in order for me to express them with my senses and express what I experience, they have to be put in some symbolic form. And it is in this form that I observe these occurrences. I'm explaining subtle, non-physical, non visible forces.

Chapter - 9

Problem solving, we claim we do, but we actually attach ourselves to the problem. That is what causes the pressure in the head. The worry and the physiological disturbances. But when thinking leads to release, often through unconscious processes, the physiological vicious cycle does not have a chance to get started. They should explain why consciously putting light around yourself might not necessarily be helpful to you at all. There are methods for putting this energy around you, and the best method is, of course, to have a normal regulated function of all the organs in your body, which means that all the chakras or subtle energy centers have to be operating at full capacity. Let us now see how these truckers are involved in the energy output of the human organism.

A practical review of the chakras. There is a great deal of misunderstanding about the chakras, about so many metaphysical systems, it is difficult to resolve the different modes of expression used to describe the chakra system. When I discuss the chakras, therefore, I am only sharing what I've observed in the thirty five years that I have been able to see the chakras and their energy and what they do in the body. I am not really so interested in the philosophical aspects, rather, I prefer to focus on the practical applications of this knowledge. I see too many people walking around absorbed in philosophy with their eyes on the sky, and it is obvious that they are deceased and they have all kinds of physiological problems.

They are starry eyed, but have a slow body that makes very little sense to me if our knowledge cannot be practical, it has little value. This is not to deny the value of the spiritual side of life, but one cannot be spiritual without the proper direction of mind and without the proper physical vehicle through which the spirit can operate. According to people who can perceive these things, the body appears to have 13 subtle energy centers called chakras. Chocolate is this desperate word for real, the word was chosen because those who are able to observe the chakras by looking through the aura see them in cross Chapter as fast moving vortices of energy containing colors. Six of the choppers are minor and their activities and seven are major, all seven major choppers except one interrelate with the endocrine system.

Remember, however, that when I mention an endocrine gland connected with a particular chakra, I'm referring not to the chakra itself, but rather to the organ that is influenced by the energy field. The choppers should be thought of as Dynamo's dynamic centers through which the energy is distributed. This energy is distributed from the Choctaws as it comes into the body as well as when it goes out of the body. There is a capacity for transmission as well as for reception, the choppers are the centers that make the area brighter and brighter or dimmer and dimmer depending on their activity. Each of the chakras vibrates at a characteristic frequency as it transmits energy, the energy pattern around each chakra is viewed as a vortex predominantly of a certain color, which corresponds to the frequency at which that chakras vibrate.

Similarly, each is associated with a musical tone that also corresponds to the frequency of its basic vibration. When a chopper is operating in a balanced manner, the color surrounding it will be very pale and it will be the pure color of that chakra. The pale color indicates that the energy transmitted by the chocolate is fine and subtle. If a chopper is not properly transmitting the energy that comes into it, the color will have a dense dark outflow that will be apparent in the aura surrounding the chopper. In my earlier book, Voluntary Controls, I discussed at some length the characteristics of each of the chakras. In brief, each aircraft has an external physical counterpart in one of the seven major glands of the body. Each has a characteristic color and frequency of the vibration associated with the quality of the energy. This concern with.

Table table one characteristics of the chakras, chakra, root or sacral spinal location for fourth, sacral vertebra, organ gonads. Color red or orange energy left promoting. Chakra spleen, spinal location, first, lumbar vertebra, organ, spleen. Color, pink, energy, reserve or love. Chakra, solar plexus, spinal location, a thoracic vertebra, organ, adrenals, color, green energy, life preserving. Chakra part. Spinal location, first, thoracic vertebra, organ blindness, color, gold, energy, mental or consciousness. Chakra throat, spinal location, third cervical vertebrae, organ, thyroid color blue. Energy expressive. Jorquera, Brout, Spinel, location first, cervical vertebra, organ, pituitary color, indigo energy synthesizing. Chopra, Crout, spinal location, none organ, color. Palpable energy integration.

The colors of the chakras are not in rainbow order. That is, the sequence of colors in the chakras from lowest to highest is not in the order of the spectrum. When we realize that each of the chakras resonate with a certain color, sound and frequency, it is easier to understand how color and sound can have a therapeutic effect. They can help to stimulate and balance the activity of particular chakras. Involuntary controls outlined a series of Chopra exercises that enabled people to check the function of each chakra through meditation and color breathing. At the Veterans Hospital in Topeka, Kansas, psychotic patients were taught to do the choker exercises every day.

Through these exercises, they were able to become calmer and their creativity was enhanced, so the Chalke exercises can be useful not only for monitoring our physiological functioning, but also to regulate our mental functioning. We know that there are physical somatic diseases, but there are some metaphysic diseases as well. That is when your body does not operate properly. You cannot do anything with it, no matter how powerful your mind is and how much you perceive it, if your mind does not have the instrument through which to express its perceptions. You are like the sculptor who has a fantastic image of a statue in his mind, but who does not have the clay or rock to chisel it out of the mental image, does not do anybody any good energy transformation through the chakras with their review of the function of the choppers in mind.

Let us return to the question of how we can nourish ourselves on pure energy on white. We shall see in Chapter two that just as there is an output of energy from the body, there's also an input which is called the ray. The bay takes the form of light and the color of the light that remains is the same for each individual throughout his lifetime. According to my personal observation, this light or current, which I've also called the rape, enters the body through the crown chakra, which is associated with the pineal gland. At this point, the energy is pure light, but as it moves down to the brow chakra, which is associated with the pituitary gland, it is broken down into seven different qualities.

The pituitary functions as a prison and breaks down the light the same way a prison breaks white light into a spectrum, the pituitary refracts the light and distributes this throughout the body by way of the various chakras. The pituitary is known as the master gland because of its role in regulating the function of the body through its hormonal secretions. As a subtle energy center, the pituitary or brow chakra plays a similar role in regulating and distributing energy. When the energy returns back up through the chuckers after it has been distributed to and utilized by the various organs and systems of the body, the brow or pituitary chakra functions as a synthesizer, integrating the component energies once again into pure white light.

After the lid has been broken down into seven different qualities by the brow chakra, it moves down to the throat chakra, which is associated with the thyroid gland. Here is the first place where the light starts to become denser so that it can interact with the body chemistry and as it goes down through the subtle energy centers, it becomes progressively denser still. A throat chakra, the seven qualities are divided into three groups, three qualities on the right, the male creative side, which deal with Annabell isn't the process of building up whereby new substances or chemistries or forms of substances are created.

Three qualities on the left, the feminine, receptive side, which deal with metabolism, the process of breaking down substances, taking them out of the form in which they entered, and one quality in the middle, the catalyst which brings immobilism and metabolism together in the total process of metabolism. These qualities of energy are used to nourish the various systems of the body with each chakra drawing out the energy it requires. I should make it clear that when I talk about energy transformations in this manner, I'm making a symbolic statement about what I actually observe.

What I perceive as multidimensional planes of consciousness and energy fields, no matter how these things may occur objectively, in order for me to express them with my senses and express what I experience, they have to be put in some symbolic form. And it is in this form that I observe these occurrences. I'm explaining subtle, non-physical, non visible forces in terms of concepts that can be communicated to others. When I see the light entering the head, I can really see it being bent by the pituitary functioning as a prism and I can really see seven main colors occurring after the light is refracted. These colors represent different levels of energies, and because consciousness is a quality of energy, I associate different levels of consciousness with these energy levels.

Of course, these phenomena have not been verified in scientific laboratories. I'm merely reporting the way I actually perceive occurrences that are not generally considered capable of being perceived because they're multidimensional in nature. To return to the chakras, the energy moves down from the throat to the heart chakra, the seat of consciousness. It is at this chakra that the light undergoes a transformation into fire, a somewhat denser energy form. Conversely, what energy moves up through the chakras? It is at the heart chakra that the denser energy is converted once again into light. Balanced at the pivotal point in the center of the seven chakras, the heart is a cauldron in which energy is transmuted, in which lower energies are purified into higher and higher energies are rendered denser so that they can nourish the physical body.

The heart chakra is associated with the Times Square, which regulates the lymphatic system of the body and governs the immunological defenses. This mysterious land, we are told by medical authorities entropies after the age of 13. This is considered normal. How can we call an atrophy England normal? Every part of our bodies has a function, it is more likely that we're failing to utilize the thymus for the function for which it was intended. I consider it no surprise that in our society, the thymus gland should atrophy at the age of 13 because it is about that age that young people are launched into adulthood, that they are told they must start worrying about how they will make a living when they grow up. What kind of person they're going to marry and so on.

Rather than make our young people aware of mental and spiritual survival, our culture emphasizes mere physical survival and from their early teens on it is their physical survival that is emphasized at the expense of their mental health and spiritual development. The heart chakra is the seat of consciousness. Little wonder, then, that the gland with which it is intimately associated should begin to atrophy at the point when we begin to neglect the development of the consciousness. No wonder either that we have such low resistance throughout our lymphatic system that we're perpetually subject to colds and flu for it is neglected thymus gland that should be giving us the protection we lack.

With this transmutation into denser form at the heart chakra, the energy moves down and activates the adrenal glands at the solar plexus chakra, then onto the spleen, pancreas and liver at the spleen chakra. These three organs begin the filtering operation, removing the waste material created in the burning process. Finally, the energy in its densest form reaches the gonadal system at the root chakra, which I like to compare to a butane tank with a pilot light on it.

Chapter - 10

Frequency of its basic vibration. When a chopper is operating in a balanced manner, the color surrounding it will be very pale and it will be the pure color of that chakra. The pale color indicates that the energy transmitted by the chakra is fine and subtle. If a chopper is not properly transmitting the energy that comes into it, the color will have a dense dark outflow that will be apparent in the aura surrounding the chakra. In my earlier book, Voluntary Controls, I discussed at some length the characteristics of each of the chakras. In brief, each aircraft has an external physical counterpart in one of the seven major glands of the body. Each has a characteristic color and frequency of the vibration associated with the quality of the energy this concern with.

Table table one characteristics of the chakras, chakra, root or sacral spinal location for fourth, sacral vertebra, organ gonads. Color red or orange energy left promoting. Chakra spleen, spinal location, first, lumbar vertebra, organ, spleen. Color, pink, energy, reserve or love. Chakra, solar plexus, spinal location, a thoracic vertebra, organ, adrenals, color, green energy, preserving. Chakra part. Spinal location, first, thoracic vertebra, organ blindness, color, gold, energy, mental or consciousness. Chakra throat, spinal location, third cervical vertebrae, organ, thyroid color blue. Energy expressive. Chakra Brout Spinel location for a cervical vertebra, organ, pituitary color, indigo energy synthesizing.

Chopra crown spinal location none, organ color, pale purple energy integration. The colors of the chakras are not in rainbow order. That is, the sequence of colors in the chakras from lowest to highest is not in the order of the spectrum. When we realize that each of the chakras resonate with a certain color, sound and frequency, it is easier to understand how color and sound can have a therapeutic effect. They can help to stimulate and balance the activity of particular chakras. Involuntary controls, I outlined a series of Chopra exercises that enabled people to check the function of each chakra through meditation and color breathing. At the Veterans Hospital in Topeka, Kansas, psychotic patients were taught to do the choker exercises every day.

Through these exercises, they were able to become calmer and their creativity was enhanced, so the Chalke exercises can be useful not only for monitoring our physiological functioning, but also to regulate our mental functioning. We know that there are somatic diseases, but there are some metaphysic diseases as well. That is when your body does not operate properly. You cannot do anything with it, no matter how powerful your mind is and how much you perceive it, if your mind does not have the instrument through which to express its perceptions. You are like the sculptor who has a fantastic image of a statue in his mind, but who does not have the clay or rock to chisel it out of the mental image, does not do anybody any good energy transformation through the chakras with their review of the function of the choppers in mind.

Let us return to the question of how we can nourish ourselves on pure energy on white. We shall see in Chapter two that just as there is an output of energy from the body, there's also an input which is called the ray. The raid takes the form of light and the color of the light that remains is the same for each individual throughout his lifetime. According to my personal observation, this slight or current, which I've also called the ray, enters the body through the crown chakra, which is associated with the pineal gland. At this point, the energy is pure light, but as it moves down to the brow chakra, which is associated with the pituitary gland, it is broken down into seven different qualities.

The pituitary functions as a prison and breaks down the light the same way a prison breaks white light into a spectrum, the pituitary refracts the light and is distributed throughout the body by way of the various chakras. The pituitary is known as the master gland because of its role in regulating the function of the body through its hormonal secretions. As a subtle energy center, the pituitary or brow chakra plays a similar role in regulating and distributing energy. When the energy returns back up through the chuckers after it has been distributed to and utilized by the various organs and systems of the body, the brow or pituitary chakra functions as a synthesizer, integrating the component energies once again into pure white light.

After the lid has been broken down into seven different qualities by the brow chakra, it moves down to the throat chakra, which is associated with the thyroid gland. Here is the first place where the light starts to become denser so that it can interact with the body chemistry and as it goes down through the subtle energy centers, it becomes progressively denser still. A throat chakra, the seven qualities are divided into three groups, three qualities on the right, the male creative side, which deal with Anabel isn't the process of building up whereby new substances or chemistries or forms of substances are created.

Three qualities on the left, the feminine, receptive side, which deal with metabolism, the process of breaking down substances, taking them out of the form in which they entered, and one quality in the middle, the catalyst which brings an embolism and catabolic them together in the total process of metabolism. These qualities of energy are used to nourish the various systems of the body with each chakra drawing out the energy it requires. I should make it clear that when I talk about energy transformations in this manner, I'm making a symbolic statement about what I actually observe.

What I perceive as multidimensional planes of consciousness and energy fields, no matter how these things may occur objectively, in order for me to express them with my senses and express what I experience, they have to be put in some symbolic form. And it is in this form that I observe these occurrences. I'm explaining subtle, non-physical, non visible forces in terms of concepts that can be communicated to others. When I see the light entering the head, I can really see it being bent by the pituitary functioning as a prism and I can really see seven main colors occurring after the light is refracted. These colors represent different levels of energies, and because consciousness is a quality of energy, I associate different levels of consciousness with these energy levels.

Of course, these phenomena have not been verified in scientific laboratories. I'm merely reporting the way I actually perceive occurrences that are not generally considered capable of being perceived because they're multidimensional in nature. To return to the chakras, the energy moves down from the throat to the heart chakra, the seat of consciousness. It is at this chakra that the light undergoes a transformation into fire, a somewhat denser energy form. Conversely, what energy moves up through the chakras? It is at the heart chakra that the denser energy is converted once again into light.

Balance at the pivotal point in the center of the seven chakras, the heart is the cauldron in which energy is transmuted, in which lower energies are purified into higher and higher energies are rendered denser so that they can nourish the physical body. The heart chakra is associated with the thymus gland, which regulates the lymphatic system of the body and governs the immunological defenses. This mysterious grand, we are told by medical authorities entropies after the age of 13. This is considered normal. How can we call an atrophy England normal? Every part of our bodies has a function, it is more likely that we're failing to utilize the thymus for the function for which it was intended.

I consider no surprise that in our society, the thymus gland should atrophy at the age of 13 because it is about that age that young people are launched into adulthood, that they are told they must start worrying about how they will make a living when they grow up. What kind of person they're going to marry and so on. Rather than make our young people aware of mental and spiritual survival, our culture emphasizes mere physical survival and from their early teens on it is their physical survival that is emphasized at the expense of their mental health and spiritual development. The heart chakra is the seat of consciousness.

Little wonder, then, that the gland with which it is intimately associated should begin to atrophy at the point when we begin to neglect the development of the consciousness. No wonder either that we have such low resistance throughout our lymphatic system that we're perpetually subject to colds and flu for it is neglected thymus gland that should be giving us the protection we lack. With this transmutation into denser form at the heart chakra, the energy moves down and activates the adrenal glands at the solar plexus chakra, then onto the spleen, pancreas and liver at the spleen chakra. These three organs begin the filtering operation, removing the waste material created in the burning process.

Finally, the energy in its densest form reaches the gonadal system at the root chakra, which I like to compare to a butane tank with a pilot light on it, because the density of the energy here is concentrated like liquid oxygen, and the energy released is released very slowly unless it is activated. As I've already said, the reverse process also takes place once the energy is provided nourishment, it is released out of its physical and chemical state and it becomes sutler and settlor until finally it once again gets to the heart chakra. The cauldron, which acts now as a refinery transmuting fire into light. The energy becomes a subtle substance once again.

And finally it comes out of the pinole. I do not mean this description to be taken in the metaphysical sense, I am talking literally about energy conversions and changes in energy states. Of course, this transformation cannot yet be proved scientifically. Nevertheless, this is what I've observed in human energies, and I feel fortunate to be able to see these energies moving and thereby, after years of observation, to get some idea of what is going on. This is the process I have observed the transmutation of light to fire the substance. And the transmutation of substance to fire, to light. Energy flow and health.

As a preceding discussion indicates, it is obvious that for an optimal utilization of energy, it is desirable for all the chakras or human energy centers to be functioning in a balanced, fully operative manner because the chakras, through their interrelation and interaction with all the endocrine glands, maintain normal function of all the body's organs. If one of the chakras slows down in its actions, if it is in a state of inertia, the energy flow is impeded and organs will begin to show signs of illness. We must remember that the choppers are never completely blocked or closed. I sometimes hear some psychics say to people, oh, dear, your throat chakra is closed, to which I'm tempted to reply. Well, when is the funeral? If one of the chakras were really closed, you would be dead.

We can think of a spinal cord which contains six of the seven chakras of the pipe in which they are placed at intervals of very fast moving pinwheels that move the energy from one place to another through the whole canal. If any one of these dynamo stops, there is no way that energy can flow through and you will not be able to exist. If imputed energy flow through the chakras is the key to optimal health, it is obvious that attitudes and fears and anxieties that impede the flow can be just as damaging as actual physical injury to an organ. One area in which the destructive effect of mistaken ideas is emotions is very apparent in the misuse and repression of sexuality. Vital physical sexual energy is associated with the root or sacral chakra. If sex is experienced only in the gonads without undergoing transformation by rising up through the chakras, the energy is kept down in the physical realm.

Chapter - 11

Monitoring our physiological functioning, but also to regulate our mental functioning. We know that there are physical somatic diseases, but there are some metaphysic diseases as well. That is when your body does not operate properly. You cannot do anything with it, no matter how powerful your mind is and how much you perceive it, if your mind does not have the instrument through which to express its perceptions. You are like the sculptor who has a fantastic image of a statue in his mind, but who does not have the clay or rock to chisel it out of the mental image, does not do anybody any good. Energy transformation through the chakras with our review of the function of the choppers in mind, let us return to the question of how we can nourish ourselves on pure energy, on light.

We shall see in Chapter two that just as there is an output of energy from the body, there's also an input which is called the ray. The raid takes the form of light and the color of the light that remains is the same for each individual throughout his lifetime. According to my personal observation, this light or current, which I've also called the rape, enters the body through the crown chakra, which is associated with the pineal gland. At this point, the energy is pure light, but as it moves down to the brow chakra, which is associated with the pituitary gland, it is broken down into seven different qualities. The pituitary functions as a prison and breaks down the light the same way a prison breaks white light into a spectrum, the pituitary refracts the light and distributes throughout the body by way of the various chakras.

The pituitary is known as the master gland because of its role in regulating the function of the body through its hormonal secretions. As a subtle energy center, the pituitary or brow chakra plays a similar role in regulating and distributing energy. When the energy returns back up through the chuckers after it has been distributed to and utilized by the various organs and systems of the body, the brow or pituitary chakra functions as a synthesizer, integrating the component energies once again into pure white light. After the lid has been broken down into seven different qualities by the brow chakra, it moves down to the throat chakra, which is associated with the thyroid gland.

Here is the first place where the light starts to become denser so that it can interact with the body chemistry and as it goes down through the subtle energy centers, it becomes progressively denser still. A throat chakra, the seven qualities are divided into three groups, three qualities on the right, the male creative side, which deal with Anabel isn't the process of building up whereby new substances or chemistries or forms of substances are created. Three qualities on the left, the feminine, receptive side which deal with tabloidism, the process of breaking down substances, taking them out of the form in which they entered, and one quality in the middle, the catalyst which brings immobilism and metabolism together in the total process of metabolism.

These qualities of energy are used to nourish the various systems of the body with each chakra drawing out the energy it requires. I should make it clear that when I talk about energy transformations in this manner, I'm making a symbolic statement about what I actually observe. What I perceive as multidimensional planes of consciousness and energy fields, no matter how these things may occur objectively, in order for me to express them with my senses and express what I experience, they have to be put in some symbolic form. And it is in this form that I observe these occurrences. I'm explaining subtle, non-physical, non visible forces in terms of concepts that can be communicated to others.

When I see the light entering the head, I can really see it being bent by the pituitary functioning as a prism and I can really see seven main colors occurring after the light is refracted. These colors represent different levels of energies, and because consciousness is a quality of energy, I associate different levels of consciousness with these energy levels. Of course, these phenomena have not been verified in scientific laboratories, I'm merely reporting the way I actually perceive occurrences that are not generally considered capable of being perceived because they're multidimensional in nature. To return to the chakras, the energy moves down from the throat to the heart chakra, the seat of consciousness.

It is at this chakra that the light undergoes a transformation into fire, a somewhat denser energy form. Conversely, what energy moves up through the chakras? It is at the heart chakra that the denser energy is converted once again into light. Balance at the pivotal point in the center of the seven chakras, the heart is the cauldron in which energy is transmuted, in which lower energies are purified into higher and higher energies are rendered denser so that they can nourish the physical body. The heart chakra is associated with the Times gland, which regulates the lymphatic system of the body and hence governs the immunological defenses. This mysterious land, we are told by medical authorities, Atropos after the age of 13.

This is considered normal. How can we call an atrophy England normal? Every part of our bodies has a function, it is more likely that we're failing to utilize the thymus for the function for which it was intended. I consider it no surprise that in our society, the thymus gland should atrophy at the age of 13 because it is about that age that young people are launched into adulthood, that they are told they must start worrying about how they will make a living when they grow up. What kind of person they're going to marry and so on. Rather than make our young people aware of mental and spiritual survival, our culture emphasizes mere physical survival and from their early teens on it is their physical survival that is emphasized at the expense of their mental health and spiritual development. The heart chakra is the seat of consciousness.

Little wonder, then, that the gland with which it is intimately associated should begin to atrophy at the point when we begin to neglect the development of the consciousness. No wonder either that we have such low resistance throughout our lymphatic system that we're perpetually subject to colds and flu for it is neglected thymus gland that should be giving us the protection we lack. With US transmutation into denser form at the heart chakra, the energy moves down and activates the adrenal glands at the solar plexus chakra, then onto the spleen, pancreas and liver at the spleen chakra. These three organs begin the filtering operation, removing the waste material created in the burning process.

Finally, the energy in its densest form reaches the gonadal system at the root chakra, which I like to compare to a butane tank with a pilot light on it, because the density of the energy here is concentrated like liquid oxygen, and the energy released is released very slowly unless it is activated. As I've already said, the reverse process also takes place once the energy is provided nourishment, it is released out of its physical and chemical state and it becomes sutler and settlor until finally it once again gets to the heart chakra. The cauldron, which acts now as a refinery transmuting fire into light. The energy becomes a subtle substance once again.

And finally it comes out of the . I do not mean this description to be taking in the metaphysical sense, I am talking literally about energy conversions and changes in energy states. Of course, this transformation cannot yet be proved scientifically. Nevertheless, this is what I've observed in human energies, and I feel fortunate to be able to see these energies moving and thereby, after years of observation, to get some idea of what is going on. This is the process I have observed the transmutation of light to fire the substance.

And the transmutation of substance to fire, to light. Energy flow and health.

As a preceding discussion indicates, it is obvious that for an optimal utilization of energy, it is desirable for all the chakras or human energy centers to be functioning in a balanced, fully operative manner because the chakras, through their interrelation and interaction with all the endocrine glands, maintain normal function of all the body's organs. If one of the choppers slows down in its actions, if it is in a state of inertia, the energy flow is impeded and organs will begin to show signs of illness. We must remember that the choppers are never completely blocked or closed. I sometimes hear some psychics say to people, oh, dear, your throat chakra is closed, to which I'm tempted to reply.

Well, when is the funeral? If one of the chakras were really closed, you would be dead. We can think of a spinal cord which contains six of the seven chakras as a pipe in which they are placed at intervals with very fast moving pinwheels that move the energy from one place to another through the whole canal. If any one of these dynamo stops, there is no way that energy can flow through and you will not be able to exist. If energy flow through the choppers is the key to optimal health, it is obvious that attitudes and fears and anxieties that impede the flow can be just as damaging as actual physical injury to an organ. One area in which the destructive effect of mistaken ideas is emotions is very apparent in the misuse and repression of sexuality.

Vital physical sexual energy is associated with the root or sacral chakra. If sex is experienced only in the gonads without undergoing transformation by rising up through the chakras, the energy is kept down in the physical realm and becomes explosive. Sexual energy is the basic life promoting energy that provides the impetus for our organism when it moves up through the chakras, it affects every dynamo allowing for holistic sexual experience. InterBook means interacting, interrelating in order to become one from the smallest particle to the total being. It is a constant balancing and merging of the male and the female, the positive and the negative, the passive and the active in each of us.

When sodium and potassium ions interact in the cells of our bodies, that is a sexual act, an act of interBook just as much as that of female and male joining together. The sodium and potassium ions in their interaction procreate. That is, they produce a new form of energy, a new electrical stimulus, which in turn activates new groups of nutrients in our body. A very high percentage of disease can be traced to representation of sexual energy. A person may be trying to be very spiritual and may repress his or her sexuality in doing so, he or she closes off the butane tank of his or her root chakra and also shuts off his or her emotions. Such a person might look and sound spiritual, but in reality, he or she is a sick person because the energy is not flowing through him or her.

Moreover, when sexuality is held back, the higher spiritual plans are affected as much as the physical because the energy can no longer be transformed into higher levels of consciousness. What is the point, then, of denying one's sexuality? For most people, this only leads to illness on the physical, mental and spiritual plains. We should not deny the animal side of our natures. Rather, we should give up the old negative values associated with it. Thou shalt not commit adultery means to me, thou shalt not adulterate thy energy. We must not leave unused any of the energy that we have been given. We're and God, when we do things without joy or involvement of the soul. Most couples are committing adultery all the time because the sex act has become a habit.

There is no way to tell any nook meaning because the communion of our bodies must be a holistic communion, drawing on vital energy to achieve a oneness at the subtlest level of our being. There must be a spontaneous oneness to achieve total communication. In all our actions, then there must be a total soul mined by the union. For many people, celibacy can lead to dullness and lack of spontaneity. Such people are not using their sexual energy. It piles up and they become not active. And emotional. Not much spirituality is possible in such a state, no matter what you do in life, if you do not put your full being into it, you are stagnating or adulterating the energy and therefore you cannot consider yourself poor or healthy.

Yogis who successfully abstain from sex learn to transmute the vital sexual energy by bringing it up through the chakras, transforming passion into compassion. If they're unable to bring this energy up and out through the pineal gland, the pineal and pituitary will atrophy, so religious celibates must not suppress or deny their sexual energy. Rather, they must learn to transmute it into energies that will help their spiritual development and that will maintain their bodies as healthy vehicles.

The key to that healthy utilization of energy is creative expression, the best protection against harmful influences and lower forms of energy is to radiate energy yourself. Do not hold back your capacities, be spontaneous and joyous and everything you do, do not compare yourself with others and worry about whether your capacities are higher or lower than theirs. Just do it for the sake of doing. Do not hold the energy back for fear that someone will not like what you do. Just keep bringing the energy up and out.

Chapter - 12

For me to express them with my senses and express what I experience, they have to be put in some symbolic form. And it is in this form that I observe these occurrences. I'm explaining subtle, non-physical, non visible forces in terms of concepts that can be communicated to others. When I see the light entering the head, I can really see it being bent by the pituitary functioning as a prism and I can really see seven main colors occurring after the light is refracted. These colors represent different levels of energies, and because consciousness is a quality of energy, I associate different levels of consciousness with these energy levels. Of course, these phenomena have not been verified in scientific laboratories.

I'm merely reporting the way I actually perceive occurrences that are not generally considered capable of being perceived because they're multidimensional in nature. To return to the chakras, the energy moves down from the throat to the heart chakra, the seat of consciousness. It is at this chakra that the light undergoes a transformation into fire, a somewhat denser energy form. Conversely, what energy moves up through the chakras? It is at the heart chakra that the denser energy is converted once again into light. Balanced at the pivotal point in the center of the seven chakras, the heart is a cauldron in which energy is transmuted, in which lower energies are purified into higher and higher energies are rendered denser so that they can nourish the physical body.

The heart chakra is associated with the Times Square, which regulates the lymphatic system of the body and governs the immunological defenses. This mysterious grand, we are told by medical authorities entropies after the age of 13. This is considered normal. How can we call an atrophy England normal? Every part of our bodies has a function, it is more likely that we're failing to utilize the thymus for the function for which it was intended. I consider it no surprise that in our society, the thymus gland should atrophy at the age of 13 because it is about that age that young people are launched into adulthood, that they are told they must start worrying about how they will make a living when they grow up.

What kind of person they're going to marry and so on. Rather than make our young people aware of mental and spiritual survival, our culture emphasizes mere physical survival and from their early teens on it is their physical survival that is emphasized at the expense of their mental health and spiritual development. The heart chakra is the seat of consciousness. Little wonder, then, that the gland with which it is intimately associated should begin to atrophy at the point when we begin to neglect the development of the consciousness. No wonder either that we have such low resistance throughout our lymphatic system that we're perpetually subject to colds and flu for it is neglected thymus gland that should be giving us the protection we lack.

With this transmutation into denser form at the heart chakra, the energy moves down and activates the adrenal glands at the solar plexus chakra, then onto the spleen, pancreas and liver at the spleen chakra. These three organs begin the filtering operation, removing the waste material created in the burning process. Finally, the energy in its densest form reaches the gonadal system at the root chakra, which I like to compare to a butane tank with a pilot light on it, because the density of the energy here is concentrated like liquid oxygen, and the energy released is released very slowly unless it is activated. As I've already said, the reverse process also takes place once the energy is provided nourishment, it is released out of its physical and chemical state and it becomes sutler and settlor until finally it once again gets to the heart chakra. The cauldron, which acts now as a refinery transmuting fire into light.

The energy becomes a subtle substance once again. And finally it comes out of the pinole. I do not mean this description to be taking in the metaphysical sense, I am talking literally about energy conversions and changes in energy states. Of course, this transformation cannot yet be proved scientifically. Nevertheless, this is what I've observed in human energies, and I feel fortunate to be able to see these energies moving and thereby, after years of observation, to get some idea of what is going on. This is the process I have observed the transmutation of light to fire the substance. And the transmutation of substance to fire, to light. Energy flow and health.

As a preceding discussion indicates, it is obvious that for an optimal utilization of energy, it is desirable for all the chakras or human energy centers to be functioning in a balanced, fully operative manner because the chakras, through their interrelation and interaction with all the endocrine glands, maintain normal function of all the body's organs. If one of the choppers slows down in its actions, if it is in a state of inertia, the energy flow is impeded and organs will begin to show signs of illness. We must remember that the choppers are never completely blocked or closed. I sometimes hear some psychics say to people, oh, dear, your throat chakra is closed, to which I'm tempted to reply.

Well, when is the funeral? If one of the chakras were really closed, you would be dead. We can think of a spinal cord which contains six of the seven chakras as a pipe in which they are placed at intervals with very fast moving pinwheels that move the energy from one place to another through the whole canal. If any one of these dynamo stops, there is no way that energy can flow through and you will not be able to exist. If an energy flow through the choppers is the key to optimal health, it is obvious that attitudes and fears and anxieties that impede the flow can be just as damaging as actual physical injury to an organ. One area in which the destructive effect of mistaken ideas is emotions is very apparent, it's in the misuse and repression of sexuality.

Vital physical sexual energy is associated with the root or sacral chakra. If sex is experienced only in the gonads without undergoing transformation by rising up through the chakras, the energy is kept down in the physical realm and becomes explosive. Sexual energy is the basic life promoting energy that provides the impetus for our organism when it moves up through the chakras, it affects every dynamo allowing for holistic sexual experience. InterBook means interacting, interrelating in order to become one from the smallest particle to the total being. It is a constant balancing and merging of the male and female, the positive and the negative, the passive and the active in each of us. When sodium and potassium ions interact in the cells of our bodies, that is a sexual act, an act of interBook just as much as that of female and male joining together.

The sodium and potassium ions in their interaction procreate. That is, they produce a new form of energy, a new electrical stimulus, which in turn activates new groups of nutrients in our body. A very high percentage of disease can be traced to representation of sexual energy. A person may be trying to be very spiritual and may repress his or her sexuality in doing so, he or she closes off the butane tank of his or her root chakra and also shuts off his or her emotions. Such a person might look and sound spiritual, but in reality, he or she is a sick person because the energy is not flowing through him or her. Moreover, when sexuality is held back, the higher spiritual plans are affected as much as the physical because the energy can no longer be transformed into higher levels of consciousness.

What is the point, then, of denying one's sexuality? For most people, this only leads to illness on the physical, mental and spiritual plains. We should not deny the animal side of our natures. Rather, we should give up the old negative values associated with it. Thou shalt not commit adultery means to me, thou shalt not adulterate thy energy. We must not leave unused any of the energy that we have been given, we're adultery and God, when we do things without joy or involvement of the soul. Most couples are committing adultery all the time because the sex act has become a habit. There is no way to tell any nook meaning because the communion of our bodies must be a holistic communion, drawing on vital energy to achieve a oneness at the subtlest level of our being.

There must be a spontaneous oneness to achieve total communication. In all our actions, then there must be a total soul mined by the union. For many people, celibacy can lead to dullness and lack of spontaneity. Such people are not using their sexual energy. It piles up and they become not active. And emotional. Not much spirituality is possible in such a state, no matter what you do in life, if you do not put your full being into it, you are stagnating or adultery the energy and therefore you cannot consider yourself poor or healthy. Yogis who successfully abstain from sex learn to transmute the vital sexual energy by bringing it up through the chakras, transforming passion into compassion.

If they're unable to bring this energy up and out through the pineal gland, the pineal and pituitary will atrophy, so religious celibates must not suppress or deny their sexual energy. Rather, they must learn to transmute it into energies that will help their spiritual development and that will maintain their bodies as healthy vehicles. The key to that healthy utilization of energy is creative expression, the best protection against harmful influences and lower forms of energy is to radiate energy yourself. Do not hold back your capacities, be spontaneous and joyous and everything you do, do not compare yourself with others and worry about whether your capacities are higher or lower than theirs.

Just do it for the sake of doing. Do not hold the energy back for fear that someone will not like what you do. Just keep bringing the energy up and out. That is your best guarantee of a healthy body input and output of the human energy self. In this brief introduction to the idea of human energy fields, it should have become clear that what we have been talking about as the measurable electromagnetic output of the human organism, the ammunition must arise from an internal source. The outflow, the human energy field around the human body, the individualized human atmosphere is dependent on the activity that takes place within the human body. We refer to this internal activity as the imminence.

Even though the human body is not necessarily causing this energy, it is certainly producing the ammunition of the energy that has been used and activated. Imminence is the activity that happens within. If there were healthy attitudes and balanced volunteer control, you do not interfere with the imminence, the activity of the individual cellular structure and beyond that atomic and subatomic structure, then there will be a resultant radiant. We are activated by our actions, this energy emanates from us and protects us and draws the nutrients from our environment unless we interfere with it by holding back. This is why it is so important to express our energy, to keep it flowing. Wherever there is an output, there has to be an input. Interestingly enough, the input does not change visibly within the whole lifecycle.

Let us take an analogy, a common light bulb. If the letter coming from the light bulb is too bright or too dim for our purposes, we can change it. We can put in a different light bulb of a higher or lower capacity. That is, we can change the output by using more or less of the available energy, but the supply of the energy does not change the current. The input remains constant. At one hundred and fifteen volts, you can plug in more and more light bulbs until finally you blow the fuses. But we humans are not likely to blow the fuses of our fuse box because we are using only about five to 10 percent of our total energy and we still have ninety five percent to go before we will ever blow out fuses. So we do not need to be too worried about that. In Chapter two, we will discuss this constant input or the rate in detail, and in Chapter three, we will look at the ORA, which is the output of human energy.

So we might think of the Aaargh as a recording. If the light bulb has been switched on and the current is now flowing into the film of the bulb, the light is actually a recording of the activity of the current that has been set free by being released from the filament. So if we see the human body as the filament of a cosmic light bulb, we will realize that what emanates from us indicates what has been activated within the filament, that ammunition becomes a tool by which we can observe what is happening in the individual. Human energies and health maintenance. The condition of health is a regulated, balanced flow of energy through the body, which, as we have said, receives its impetus from the chakras.

Moreover, there is radiant energy emitted by the body, and this radiant electromagnetic energy is a specific relation to the location and intensity of the activity within the body. When we realized that in the final analysis of our bodies are in fact made up of nothing but energy and cost of transformation, it is easier to understand how subtle, non-physical, energetic influences such as emotions and thoughts can have a direct influence on our physical functioning, just as our physical functioning can have an effect on our emotional and mental experiences. Similarly, once we understand what produces the radio.

Chapter - 13

And with a pilot light on it, because the density of the energy here is concentrated like liquid oxygen and the energy released is released very slowly unless it is activated. As I've already said, the reverse process also takes place once the energy is provided nourishment, it is released out of its physical and chemical state and it becomes sutler and settlor until finally it once again gets to the heart chakra. The cauldron, which acts now as a refinery transmuting fire into light. The energy becomes a subtle substance once again. And finally it comes out of the . I do not mean this description to be taking in the metaphysical sense, I am talking literally about energy conversions and changes in energy states. Of course, this transformation cannot yet be proved scientifically.

Nevertheless, this is what I've observed in human energies, and I feel fortunate to be able to see these energies moving and thereby, after years of observation, to get some idea of what is going on. This is the process I have observed the transmutation of light to fire the substance. And the transmutation of substance to fire, to light. Energy flow and health. As a preceding discussion indicates, it is obvious that for an optimal utilization of energy, it is desirable for all the chakras or human energy centers to be functioning in a balanced, fully operative manner because the chakras, through their interrelation and interaction with all the endocrine glands, maintain normal function of all the body's organs. If one of the chakras slows down in its actions, if it is in a state of inertia, the energy flow is impeded and organs will begin to show signs of illness.

We must remember that the choppers are never completely blocked or closed. I sometimes hear some psychics say to people, oh, dear, your throat chakra is closed, to which I'm tempted to reply. Well, when is the funeral? If one of the chakras were really closed, you would be dead. We can think of a spinal cord which contains six of the seven chakras as a pipe in which they are placed at intervals with very fast moving pinwheels that move the energy from one place to another through the whole canal. If any one of these dynamo stops, there is no way that energy can flow through and you will not be able to exist. If energy flow through the Chapters is the key to optimal health, it is obvious that attitudes and fears and anxieties that impede the flow can be just as damaging as actual physical injury to an organ.

One area in which the destructive effect of mistaken ideas is emotions is very apparent in the misuse and repression of sexuality. Vital physical sexual energy is associated with the root or sacral chakra. If sex is experienced only in the gonads without undergoing transformation by rising up through the chakras, the energy is kept down in the physical realm and becomes explosive. Sexual energy is the basic life promoting energy that provides the impetus for our organism when it moves up through the chakras, it affects every Dinamo allowing for holistic sexual experience. InterBook means interacting, interrelating in order to become one from the smallest particle to the total being. It is a constant balancing and merging of the male and the female, the positive and the negative, the passive and the active in each of us.

When sodium and potassium ions interact in the cells of our bodies, that is a sexual act, an act of interBook just as much as that of female and male joining together. The sodium and potassium ions in their interaction procreate. That is, they produce a new form of energy, a new electrical stimulus, which in turn activates new groups of nutrients in our body. A very high percentage of disease can be traced to representation of sexual energy. A person may be trying to be very spiritual and may repress his or her sexuality in doing so, he or she closes off the butane tank of his or her root chakra and also shuts off his or her emotions. Such a person might look and sound spiritual, but in reality, he or she is a sick person because the energy is not flowing through him or her.

Moreover, when sexuality is held back, the higher spiritual plans are affected as much as the physical because the energy can no longer be transformed into higher levels of consciousness. What is the point, then, of denying one's sexuality? For most people, this only leads to illness on the physical, mental and spiritual plains, we should not deny the animal side of our natures. Rather, we should give up the old negative values associated with it. Thou shalt not commit adultery means to me, thou shalt not adulterate thy energy. We must not leave unused any of the energy that we have been given. We're and God, when we do things without joy or involvement of the soul. Most couples are committing adultery all the time because the sex act has become a habit.

There is no way to tell any nook meaning because the communion of our bodies must be a holistic communion, drawing on vital energy to achieve a oneness at the subtlest level of our being. There must be a spontaneous oneness to achieve total communication. In all our actions, then there must be a total soul mined by the union for many people, the US can lead to dullness and lack of spontaneity. Such people are not using their sexual energy. It piles up and they become not active. And emotional. Not much spirituality is possible in such a state, no matter what you do in life, if you do not put your full being into it, you are stagnating or adultery the energy and therefore you cannot consider yourself poor or healthy.

Yogis who successfully abstain from sex learn to transmute the vital sexual energy by bringing it up through the chakras, transforming passion into compassion. If they're unable to bring this energy up and out through the pineal gland, the pineal and pituitary will atrophy, so religious celibates must not suppress or deny their sexual energy. Rather, they must learn to transmute it into energies that will help their spiritual development and that will maintain their bodies as healthy vehicles. The key to that healthy utilization of energy is creative expression, the best protection against harmful influences and lower forms of energy is to radiate energy yourself. Do not hold back your capacities, be spontaneous and joyous and everything you do, do not compare yourself with others and worry about whether your capacities are higher or lower than theirs.

Just do it for the sake of doing. Do not hold the energy back for fear that someone will not like what you do, just keep bringing the energy up and out, that is your best guarantee of a healthy body input and output of the human energy self. In this brief introduction to the idea of human energy, fields should become clear that what we have been talking about as the measurable electromagnetic output of the human organism, the ammunition must arise from an internal source. The outflow, the human energy field around the human body, the individualized human atmosphere is dependent on the activity that takes place within the human body. We refer to this internal activity as the imminence.

Even though the human body is not necessarily causing this energy, it is certainly producing the ammunition of the energy that has been used and activated. Imminence is the activity that happens within. If there were healthy attitudes and balanced volunteer control, you do not interfere with the imminence, the activity of the individual cellular structure and beyond that, the atomic and subatomic structure, then there will be a resultant radiance. We are activated by our actions, this energy emanates from us and protects us and draws the nutrients from our environment unless we interfere with it by holding back. This is why it is so important to express our energy, to keep it flowing.

Wherever there is an output, there has to be an input. Interestingly enough, the input does not change visibly within the whole lifecycle. Let us take an analogy, a common light bulb. If the light from the light bulb is too bright or too dim for our purposes, we can change it. We can put in a different light bulb of a higher or lower capacity. That is, we can change the output by using more or less of the available energy, but the supply of the energy does not change the current. The input remains constant. At one hundred and fifteen volts, you can plug in more and more light bulbs until finally you blow the fuses. But we humans are not likely to blow the fuses of our fuse box because we are using only about five to 10 percent of our total energy and we still have ninety five percent to go before we will ever blow out fuses.

So we do not need to be too worried about that. In Chapter two, we will discuss this constant impact or the rate in detail, and then Chapter three, we will look at the opera, which is the output of human energy. So we might think of the opera as a recording. If the light bulb has been switched on and the current is now flowing into the filament of the bulb. The light is actually a recording of the activity of the current that has been set free by being released from the filament. So if we see the human body as the filament of a cosmic light bulb, we will realize that what emanates from us indicates what has been activated within the filament, that ammunition becomes a tool by which we can observe what is happening in the individual.

Human energies and health maintenance. The condition of health is a regulated, balanced flow of energy through the body, which, as we have said, receives its impetus from the chakras. Moreover, there is radiant energy emitted by the body, and this radiant electromagnetic energy is a specific relation to the location and intensity of the activity within the body. When we realized that in the final analysis of our bodies are in fact made up of nothing but energy and cost of transformation, it is easier to understand how subtle, non-physical, energetic influences such as emotions and thoughts can have a direct influence on our physical functioning, just as our physical functioning can have an effect on our emotional and mental experiences.

Similarly, once we understand what produces the radiant ammunition from our bodies, it is clearer why this ammunition should reveal something about the state of our functioning. What may come as more of a surprise to you is that you do not need to be psychic to benefit from the information available from observing these human energy fields. Many classes I've taught have amply demonstrated that with the proper motivation, accompanied by meditation and the eye exercises I will describe in Chapter four, people with no particular psychic gifts can learn to see the rate and the aura.

This information can be of tremendous aid to people whose lives are dedicated to counseling others or to treating others for physical illness because its subtle energy fields that surround the human body can advance warnings of problems that may not yet have manifested themselves on the physical plane. And in any case, an understanding of these energy fields can aid in a clear perception of what is really amiss in a case of mental, emotional or physical illness. Looking at the human being as an energy cell also helps us understand the roles that various sorts of nutrients play in maintaining our healthy functioning.

One Chapter I will be repeating throughout this book is that it is not enough to have a healthy diet or to take certain vitamins and minerals and herbs. Organisms must be able to assimilate these nutrients in order for them to do us any good. In Chapter five, I will share my understanding of this process of assimilation, of how we attract nutrients we require from our environment, and of how this is related to the healing properties of birds, colors, sounds, minerals, cell salts and other therapeutic agents. In Chapter six, I will describe a system I've been using successfully for many years that integrates all these diverse ways of dealing with the regulation of human energies.

The purpose of this focus on health is, Of course, not to simply maintain the physical body in proper functioning order, although that is a very important goal fundamental to the higher purposes we are pursuing. It is only through the proper functioning of our physical vehicle, the body and the balanced, integrated functioning of our emotions, which are interdependent with the physical body, that we can begin to liberate and express the energies that come through the vehicle of the mind and finally lead to manifestation of the soul, the spirit, the total energetic essence that is you as an individual, as part of the cosmos.

Chapter - 14

Balancing and merging of the male and female, the positive and the negative, the passive and the active in each of us. When sodium and potassium ions interact in the cells of our bodies, that is a sexual act, an act of interBook just as much as that of female and male joining together. The sodium and potassium ions in their interaction procreate. That is, they produce a new form of energy, a new electrical stimulus, which in turn activates new groups of nutrients in our body. A very high percentage of disease can be traced to representation of sexual energy. A person may be trying to be very spiritual and may repress his or her sexuality in doing so, he or she closes off the butane tank of his or her root chakra and also shuts off his or her emotions.

Such a person might look and sound spiritual, but in reality, he or she is a sick person because the energy is not flowing through him or her. Moreover, when sexuality is held back, the higher spiritual plans are affected as much as the physical because the energy can no longer be transformed into higher levels of consciousness. What is the point, then, of denying one's sexuality? For most people, this only leads to illness on the physical, mental and spiritual plains, we should not deny the animal side of our natures. Rather, we should give up the old negative values associated with it. Thou shalt not commit adultery means to me, thou shalt not adulterate thy energy.

We must not leave unused any of the energy that we have been given. Are adults and God, when we do things without joy or involvement of the soul. Most couples are committing adultery all the time because the sex act has become a habit. There is no way to tell any nook meaning because the communion of our bodies must be a holistic communion, drawing on vital energy to achieve a oneness at the subtlest level of our being. There must be a spontaneous oneness to achieve total communication. In all our actions, then there must be a total soul mined by the union. For many people, celibacy can lead to dullness and lack of spontaneity. Such people are not using their sexual energy. It piles up and they become not active. And emotional.

Not much spirituality is possible in such a state, no matter what you do in life, if you do not put your full being into it, you are stagnating or adultery the energy and therefore you cannot consider yourself poor or healthy. Yogis who successfully abstain from sex learn to transmute the vital sexual energy by bringing it up through the chakras, transforming passion into compassion. If they're unable to bring this energy up and out through the pineal gland, the pineal and pituitary will atrophy, so religious celibates must not suppress or deny their sexual energy. Rather, they must learn to transmute it into energies that will help their spiritual development and that will maintain their bodies as healthy vehicles.

The key to that healthy utilization of energy is creative expression, the best protection against harmful influences and lower forms of energy is to radiate energy yourself. Do not hold back your capacities, be spontaneous and joyous and everything you do, do not compare yourself with others and worry about whether your capacities are higher or lower than theirs. Just do it for the sake of doing. Do not hold the energy back for fear that someone will not like what you do. Just keep bringing the energy up and out. That is your best guarantee of a healthy body input and output of the human energy self.

In this brief introduction to the idea of human energy fields, it should have become clear that what we have been talking about as the measurable electromagnetic output of the human organism, the ammunition must arise from an internal source. The outflow, the human energy fields around the human body, individualized human atmosphere is dependent on the activity that takes place within the human body. We refer to this internal activity as the imminence. Even though the human body is not necessarily causing this energy, it is certainly producing the ammunition of the energy that has been used and activated. Imminence is the activity that happens within.

If there were healthy attitudes and balanced volunteer control, you do not interfere with the imminence, the activity of the individual cellular structure and beyond that, the atomic and subatomic structure, then there will be a resultant radiance. We are activated by our actions, this energy emanates from us and protects us and draws the nutrients from our environment unless we interfere with it by holding back. This is why it is so important to express our energy, to keep it flowing. Wherever there is an output, there has to be an input. Interestingly enough, the input does not change visibly within the whole lifecycle.

Let us take an analogy, a common light bulb. If the light that comes from a light bulb is too bright or too dim for our purposes, we can change it. We can put in a different light bulb of a higher or lower capacity. That is, we can change the output by using more or less of the available energy, but the supply of the energy does not change the current. The input remains constant. At one hundred and fifteen volts, you can plug in more and more light bulbs until finally you blow the fuses. But we humans are not likely to blow the fuses of our fuse box because we are using only about five to 10 percent of our total energy and we still have ninety five percent to go before we will ever blow out fuses. So we do not need to be too worried about that.

In Chapter two, we will discuss this constant impact or the rate in detail, and in Chapter three, we will look at the ORA, which is the output of the human energy cell. We might think of the aura as a recording if the light bulb has been switched on and the current is now flowing into the filament of the bulb. The light is actually a recording of the activity of the current that has been set free by being released from the filament. So if we see the human body as the filament of a cosmic light bulb, we will realize that what emanates from us indicates what has been activated within the filament, that ammunition becomes a tool by which we can observe what is happening in the individual. Human energies and health maintenance.

The condition of health is a regulated, balanced flow of energy through the body, which, as we have said, receives its impetus from the chakras. Moreover, there is radiant energy emitted by the body, and this radiant electromagnetic energy is a specific relation to the location and intensity of the activity within the body. When we realized that in the final analysis of our bodies are in fact made up of nothing but energy and cost of transformation, it is easier to understand how subtle, non-physical, energetic influences such as emotions and thoughts can have a direct influence on our physical functioning, just as our physical functioning can have an effect on our emotional and mental experiences.

Similarly, once we understand what produces the radiant ammunition from our bodies, it is clear why this ammunition should reveal something about the state of our functioning. What may come as more of a surprise to you is that you do not need to be psychic to benefit from the information available from observing these human energy fields. Many classes I've taught have amply demonstrated that with the proper motivation, accompanied by meditation and the eye exercises I will describe in Chapter four, people with no particular psychic gifts can learn to see the rate and the aura.

This information can be of tremendous aid to people whose lives are dedicated to counseling others or to treating others for physical illness because its subtle energy fields that surround the human body can advance warning of problems that may not yet have manifested themselves on the physical plane. And in any case, an understanding of these energy fields can aid in a clear perception of what is really amiss in a case of mental, emotional or physical illness. Looking at the human being as an energy cell also helps us understand the roles that various sorts of nutrients play in maintaining our healthy functioning. One Chapter I will be repeating throughout this book is that it is not enough to have a healthy diet or to take certain vitamins and minerals and herbs. Organisms must be able to assimilate these nutrients in order for them to do us any good.

In Chapter five, I will share my understanding of this process of assimilation, of how we attract nutrients we require from our environment, and of how this is related to the healing properties of herbs, colors, sounds, minerals, salt and other therapeutic agents. In Chapter six, I will describe a system I've been using successfully for many years that integrates all these diverse ways of dealing with the regulation of human energies. The purpose of this focus on health is, Of course, not to simply maintain the physical body in proper functioning order, although that is a very important goal fundamental to the higher purposes we are pursuing.

It is only through the proper functioning of our physical vehicle, the body and the balanced, integrated functioning of our emotions, which are interdependent with the physical body, that we can begin to liberate and express the energies that come through the vehicle of the mind and finally lead to manifestation of the soul, the spirit, the total energetic essence that is you as an individual, as part of the cosmos.

Chapter - 15

Is creative expression the best protection against harmful influences and lower forms of energy is to radiate energy yourself. Do not hold back your capacities, be spontaneous and joyous and everything you do, do not compare yourself with others and worry about whether your capacities are higher or lower than theirs. Just do it for the sake of doing. Do not hold the energy back for fear that someone will not like what you do. Just keep bringing the energy up and out. That is your best guarantee of a healthy body input and output of the human energy self. In this brief introduction to the idea of human energy fields, it should become clear that what we have been talking about as the measurable electromagnetic output of the human organism, the ammunition must arise from an internal source.

The outflow, the human energy fields around the human body, the individualized human atmosphere is dependent on the activity that takes place within the human body. We refer to this internal activity as the imminence. Even though the human body is not necessarily causing this energy, it is certainly producing the ammunition of the energy that has been used and activated. Imminence is the activity that happens within. If there were healthy attitudes and balanced volunteer control, you do not interfere with the imminence, the activity of the individual cellular structure and beyond that, the atomic and subatomic structure, then there will be a resultant radiance.

We are activated by our actions, this energy emanates from us and protects us and draws the nutrients from our environment unless we interfere with it by holding back. This is why it is so important to express our energy, to keep it flowing. Wherever there is an output, there has to be an input. Interestingly enough, the input does not change visibly within the whole lifecycle. Let us take an analogy, a common light bulb. If the light from the light bulb is too bright or too dim for our purposes, we can change it. We can put in a different light bulb of a higher or lower capacity. That is, we can change the output by using more or less of the available energy, but the supply of the energy does not change the current.

The input remains constant. At one hundred and fifteen volts, you can plug in more and more light bulbs until finally you blow the fuses. But we humans are not likely to blow the fuses of our fuse box because we are using only about five to 10 percent of our total energy and we still have ninety five percent to go before we will ever blow out fuses. So we do not need to be too worried about that. In Chapter two, we will discuss this constant input or the rate in detail, and then Chapter three, we will look at the opera, which is the output of the human energy cell. We might think of the aura as a recording if the light bulb has been switched on and the current is now flowing into the filament of the bulb, the light is actually a recording of the activity of the current that has been set free by being released from the filament.

So if we see the human body as the filament of a cosmic light bulb, we will realize that what emanates from us indicates what has been activated within the filament, that ammunition becomes a tool by which we can observe what is happening in the individual. Human energies and health maintenance. The condition of health is a regulated, balanced flow of energy through the body, which, as we have said, receives its impetus from the chakras. Moreover, there is radiant energy emitted by the body, and this radiant electromagnetic energy is a specific relation to the location and intensity of the activity within the body.

When we realized that in the final analysis of our bodies are in fact made up of nothing but energy and cost of transformation, it is easier to understand how subtle, non-physical, energetic influences such as emotions and thoughts can have a direct influence on our physical functioning, just as our physical functioning can have an effect on our emotional and mental experiences. Similarly, once we understand what produces the radiant ammunition from our bodies, it is clearer why this ammunition should reveal something about the state of our functioning. What may come as more of a surprise to you is that you do not need to be psychic to benefit from the information available from observing these human energy fields.

Many classes I've taught have amply demonstrated that with the proper motivation, accompanied by meditation and the eye exercises I will describe in Chapter four, people with no particular psychic gifts can learn to see the rate and the aura. This information can be of tremendous aid to people whose lives are dedicated to counseling others or to treating others for physical illness because subtle energy fields that surround the human body can advance warnings of problems that may not yet have manifested themselves on the physical plane. And in any case, an understanding of these energy fields can aid in a clear perception of what is really amiss in a case of mental, emotional or physical illness.

Looking at the human being as an energy cell also helps us understand the roles that various sorts of nutrients play in maintaining our healthy functioning. One Chapter I will be repeating throughout this book is that it is not enough to have a healthy diet or to take certain vitamins and minerals and herbs. Organisms must be able to assimilate these nutrients in order for them to do us any good. In Chapter five, I will share my understanding of this process of assimilation, of how we attract nutrients we require from our environment, and of how this is related to the healing properties of birds, colors, sounds, minerals, soil salts and other therapeutic agents.

In Chapter six, I will describe a system I've been using successfully for many years that integrates all these diverse ways of dealing with the regulation of human energies. The purpose of this focus on health is, Of course, not to simply maintain the physical body in proper functioning order, although that is a very important goal fundamental to the higher purposes we are pursuing. It is only through the proper functioning of our physical vehicle, the body and the balanced, integrated functioning of our emotions, which are interdependent with the physical body, that we can begin to liberate and express the energies that come through the vehicle of the mind and finally lead to manifestation of the soul, the spirit, the total energetic essence that is you as an individual, as part of the cosmos.

Bob is too bright or too dim for our purposes, we can change it, we can put in a different light bulb of a higher or lower capacity. That is, we can change the output by using more or less of the available energy, but the supply of the energy does not change the current. The input remains constant. At one hundred and fifteen volts, you can plug in more and more light bulbs until finally you blow the fuses. But we humans are not likely to blow the fuses of our fuse box because we are using only about five to 10 percent of our total energy and we still have ninety five percent to go before we will ever blow out fuses. So we do not need to be too worried about that.

In Chapter two, we will discuss this cost and impact or the rate in detail, and then Chapter three, we will look at the opera, which is the output of the human energy self. We might think of the aura as a recording if the light bulb has been switched on and the current is now flowing into the filament of the bulb. The light is actually a recording of the activity of the current that has been set free by being released from the filament. So if we see the human body as the filament of a cosmic light bulb, we will realize that what emanates from us indicates what has been activated within the filament, that ammunition becomes a tool by which we can observe what is happening in the individual.

Human energies and health maintenance. The condition of health is a regulated, balanced flow of energy through the body, which, as we have said, receives its impetus from the chakras. Moreover, there is radiant energy emitted by the body, and this radiant electromagnetic energy is a specific relation to the location and intensity of the activity within the body. When we realize that in the final analysis of our bodies are in fact made up of nothing but energy and cost of transformation, it is easier to understand how subtle, non-physical, energetic influences such as emotions and thoughts can have a direct influence on our physical functioning, just as our physical functioning can have an effect on our emotional and mental experiences.

Similarly, once we understand what produces the radiant ammunition from our bodies, it is clear why this ammunition should reveal something about the state of our functioning. What may come as more of a surprise to you is that you do not need to be psychic to benefit from the information available from observing these human energy fields. Many classes I've taught have amply demonstrated that with the proper motivation, accompanied by meditation and the eye exercises I will describe in Chapter four, people with no particular psychic gifts can learn to see the rate and the aura.

This information can be of tremendous aid to people whose lives are dedicated to counseling others or to treating others for physical illness because subtle energy fields that surround the human body can advance warnings of problems that may not yet have manifested themselves on the physical plane. And in any case, an understanding of these energy fields can aid in a clear perception of what is really amiss in a case of mental, emotional or physical illness. Looking at the human being as an energy cell also helps us understand the roles that various sorts of nutrients play in maintaining our healthy functioning.

One Chapter I will be repeating throughout this book is that it is not enough to have a healthy diet or to take certain vitamins and minerals and herbs. Organisms must be able to assimilate these nutrients in order for them to do us any good. In Chapter five, I will share my understanding of this process of assimilation, of how we attract nutrients we require from our environment, and of how this is related to the healing properties of birds, colors, sounds, minerals, soil salts and other therapeutic agents. In Chapter six, I will describe a system I've been using successfully for many years that integrates all these diverse ways of dealing with the regulation of human energies.

The purpose of this focus on health is, Of course, not to simply maintain the physical body in proper functioning order, although that is a very important goal fundamental to the higher purposes we are pursuing. It is only through the proper functioning of our physical vehicle, the body and the balanced, integrated functioning of our emotions, which are interdependent with the physical body, that we can begin to liberate and express the energies that come through the vehicle of the mind and finally lead to manifestation of the soul, the spirit, the total energetic essence that is you as an individual, as part of the cosmos.

Chapter - 16

Happening in the individual human energies and health maintenance, the condition of health is a regulated, balanced flow of energy through the body, which, as we have said, receives its impetus from the chakras. Moreover, there is radiant energy emitted by the body, and this radiant electromagnetic energy is a specific relation to the location and intensity of the activity within the body. When we realize that in the final analysis of our bodies are in fact made up of nothing but energy and constant transformation, it is easier to understand how subtle, non-physical, energetic influences such as emotions and thoughts can have a direct influence on our physical functioning, just as our physical functioning can have an effect on our emotional and mental experiences.

Similarly, once we understand what produces the radiant ammunition from our bodies, it is clearer why this ammunition should reveal something about the state of our functioning. What may come as more of a surprise to you is that you do not need to be psychic to benefit from the information available from observing these human energy fields, many Books I've taught have amply demonstrated that with the proper motivation, accompanied by meditation and the eye exercises I will describe in Chapter four, people with no particular psychic gifts can learn to see the rate and the aura.

This information can be of tremendous aid to people whose lives are dedicated to counseling others or to treating others for physical illness because subtle energy fields that surround the human body can advance warning of problems that may not yet have manifested themselves on the physical plane. And in any case, an understanding of these energy fields can aid in a clear perception of what is really amiss in a case of mental, emotional or physical illness. Looking at the human being as an energy cell also helps us understand the roles that various sorts of nutrients play in maintaining our healthy functioning.

One Chapter I will be repeating throughout this book is that it is not enough to have a healthy diet or to take certain vitamins and minerals and herbs. Organisms must be able to assimilate these nutrients in order for them to do us any good in Chapter five. I will share my understanding of this process of assimilation, of how we attract nutrients we require from our environment, and of how this is related to the healing properties of herbs, colors, sounds, minerals, soil, salts and other therapeutic agents. In Chapter six, I will describe a system I've been using successfully for many years that integrates all these diverse ways of dealing with the regulation of human energies.

The purpose of this focus on health is, Of course, not to simply maintain the physical body in proper functioning order, although that is a very important goal fundamental to the higher purposes we are pursuing. It is only through the proper functioning of our physical vehicle, the body and the balanced, integrated functioning of our emotions, which are interdependent with the physical body that we can begin to liberate and express the energies that come through the vehicle of the mind and finally lead to manifestation of the soul, the spirit, the total energetic essence that is you as an individual, as part of the cosmos.

One thing I will be repeating throughout this book is that it is not enough to have a healthy diet or to take certain vitamins and minerals and herbs. Organisms must be able to assimilate these nutrients in order for them to do us any good in Chapter five. I will share my understanding of this process of assimilation, of how we attract nutrients we require from our environment, and of how this is related to the healing properties of herbs, colors, sound minerals, salt salts and other therapeutic agents. In Chapter six, I will describe a system I've been using successfully for many years that integrates all these diverse ways of dealing with the regulation of human energies.

The purpose of this focus on health is, Of course, not to simply maintain the physical body in proper functioning order, although that is a very important goal fundamental to the higher purposes we are pursuing. It is only through the proper functioning of our physical vehicle, the body and the balanced, integrated functioning of our emotions, which are interdependent with the physical body that we can begin to liberate and express the energies that come through the vehicle of the mind and finally lead to manifestation of the soul, the spirit, the total energetic essence that is you as an individual, as part of the cosmos.

Chapter - 17

To raise. In the human energy cell, the impetus called the rate and the output is known as the aura. The ratios of persons, potentials and purposes and our displays, his or her present and past experiences. Because each of us is unique every day and every hour are different, even though all races and auras are formed from combinations of the three primary colors as expressed and blended by the seven chakras. There are seven different races that may be found in different combinations in different people. Before we discuss the qualities of the seven principal races, let us examine how the race is created. The origin of the ray. If you recall the light bulb analogy in Chapter one, you will remember that there is a current of electromagnetic energy that enters us through the pineal gland and is then distributed throughout the body.

This current activates the body, which begins to radiate. The process is very much like switching on a lamp, which then manifests the energy. Current. Each of us is activated by the same energy current, but each of us therefore expresses that same energy in a unique way, depending on our own different experiences. This current is the ray, which is a metaphysical term for a purely physical phenomenon. The incoming current looks like a vortex or a cone, the rain or current is essentially pure white light, but it starts to change color as soon as it hits the human atmosphere in the region of the causal aura. The cause of aura is ammunition from the human organism, and it affects the white light of the rain.

In a way, you could say that there is a rainbow effect, the density or vibration of the aura functions as a prison and refracts light. Different frequencies are separated out and different colors result. Everything that your particular energy field has experienced through the ages has produced patterns in your ammunition or aura. These patterns exist as particle waves of light of varying frequencies and amplitude. This pattern absorbs from the white light of the current, all the frequencies that correspond to it on the principle that like, attracts like. What remains is everything that your energy capacity has not yet experienced. Imagine that I have a prison and that I sent a ray of white light through it, let us assume that the combined frequency of this total thousand cycles per second.

The prison will reflect the light into seven different colors or qualities. What frequency is present now? What was one thousand cycles per second when it entered the prison has been subdivided into seven different frequencies that together total one thousand cycles per second. If I place a green absorbing screen in front of the seven colored beams, what will happen? Green has a frequency of about three hundred and fifty cycles per second, so the green screen will absorb three hundred and fifty cycles per second out of a thousand cycles per second. What we then have left is six hundred and fifty cycles per second. Now we put a red screen beyond the green one.

Red has a frequency of approximately two hundred and sixty kbps, and the screen absorbs and attracts its own vibratory rate as only three hundred and ninety six emerge from the red screen. Vibrating us three hundred and ninety kbps is the color blue. Although the incoming color was white, the color scene at the end is blue because the other colors have been filtered out. Similarly, the color scene the day after it hits the human atmosphere is determined by the screening effect of the aura. In Chapter three, the origin and dynamics of the various arc fields surrounding the body will be fully discussed. At present, it is only necessary that you understand that the aura is the storehouse of your past experiences.

These experiences have been translated into different frequencies of energy. When the white light current comes into contact with these energy patterns, the principle of like attracts like old. The remaining current of unabsorbed energy represents the experiences you have not yet had, thus the color of this row reveals the potentials within you that you're striving to be actualized in this lifetime. The rate which remains the same throughout this lifetime, shows you the tools in your toolbox, the only change that occurs in the rate is that it will become paler and hue as you use your tools. The currents will look more subtle because it is more active if you do not use these potentials, the very remains as dense as it began and the color will be dark when you activate the energy it represents.

The ray becomes sidler because you do not hold it back, but rather keep it flowing in and out. For an example, let us imagine a block of houses that are all on one hundred and fifteen volt current. One house is brightly illuminated by the many lights that are shining inside and beautiful sounds are coming from it, every little bit of the one hundred and fifty in what is being used. But in the house next door, there is just one little light glowing in the front room. Both houses have the same potential, but one is not putting that energy to work. Similarly, having a beautiful input does not necessarily imply having a beautiful output. It depends on your use of the potentials inherent in that flowing current called the ray.

Most of the time, when people say they see a certain color around you, they are really seeing not your aura, but you're right, which is brighter because it is the totality of all of your input, because you do not use all your input. Your output is never as bright. The rate in counseling. The color of the red can help us perceive our purposes and to discover our inner potentials for achieving those purposes. This is an important insight because many people never understand their purpose in being alive and are never able to find deep satisfaction in their activities. We often cling to the set patterns in our lives and fail to realize that our greatest potentials or tools are going unused.

I'm amazed to observe the wonderful capacities in some people's input while at the same time seeing hardly anything coming out of them. Based on my personal observation, it appears that most people are involved in pursuing the wrong goals and are trapped in inappropriate situations. They are fighting against themselves every day and thinking to themselves, I know I shouldn't be wasting my energy on things I'm doing, but I don't have the courage to change it. It takes great courage for someone to let go of what he or she has in order to attain a more fulfilling existence, because this new life cannot be seen until the old life is sacrificed.

Most people do not dare to bring out their potential and they keep hanging on to something with which they are completely dissatisfied. I feel that if we become aware of the dominant purpose of our lives, which is revealed by the raids we're working on, then we become much more capable of resolving our hangups and our problems. We're then encouraged to be what we were born to be. Each of us has an individual function in the universal order of things. One of the most important questions people can ask themselves is what is my purpose? It is a sad thing if they do not discover that purpose until they're very old.

In my counseling work, I find it rewarding when a mother brings her just one child to me and we can observe the baby's rate. We can learn what an infant is capable of becoming, what all its attributes and potentials are, what knowledge the child can be encouraged to develop desires consistent with its inborn purpose. Without such knowledge of our particular potentials and purposes, society gets a hold on us and often dictates our goals and activities, telling us that such and such an activity is most worthwhile because it will enable us to make more money or to have more power. If at a later age, we finally become aware of our true purposes, we feel we have wasted a lot of time.

The rain is obviously a powerful tool in counseling. It is the main area I use in my own counseling work. Because they're not fulfilling their given potentials, many people are emotionally and physically disturbed. Once they are helped to recognize their true potentials, they can understand how they have been working against themselves. Of course, knowing the color of the race is only one means of beginning to fulfill individual potentials. There are many, many types of personal introspection, contemplation and exploration that will also help us in our efforts to know ourselves. It is only through such self knowledge that we can achieve the growth and harmony better. The purpose of life, the right and the are special tools in this quest.

Types of raids. I've observed that there are seven principal rays and four forms in which those rays may appear. Of course, a ray can be a single color, in which case we simply refer to it as a ray or a single ray. Frequently there is not a single color, but is formed by a main rate and a subgroup, such an array might show, for example, 70 percent of one color and 30 percent of another color. When the main was surrounded by the subway, the subway was the one that was more active because it was open to environmental stimulation. However, even though their main route is hidden from view, it is still potent because it expresses the majority of the energy of the current.

In contrast, when the submarines are in the center of the main way, it is often repressed. That is why it is often difficult to get to know people with this type of. You can get only so far in your acquaintance with them and suddenly you hit an obstacle. You know there is more to them, but you cannot gain access to a part of them. The submarine they have not yet activated. And sometimes the individual may be rather difficult to reach even when both ways are activated. My own rate is 70 percent pink on the inside, the sub, right on the outside is blue. Pink is the way of service. It is the cosmic dressing or nourishing ray pink ray. People always feel compelled to serve others.

It is a very highly emotional rate because it is red, which is vital energy and white, which is all energy merged together. So does a life promoting color surrounding pink. In my right is blue and blue is the color of volition or willpower or cool authority. In my case, I can get highly emotional and start to exaggerate and blow things out of proportion because that excitable pink drives me to make sure I get the picture across. If I become emotional, I jokingly say to myself, oh, my pink slip is showing, I left my blue hat at home. Immediately, I put my blue hat on and mellow and control the high emotion because I become the disciplinarian and discipline starts to direct this excitable life promoting energy.

The blue right then is actually like my voltage regulator, yet there are other days when I catch myself becoming a power theory, then I say, Oh, I have my blue head, but I'm naked. So I had better put my pink slip on. Then I have to mellow this harsh, authoritarian, dictatorial attitude with service and compassion. This can give you an idea of how the qualities in the race can be used as tools. Now, a person who had blue on the inside and pink on the outside would have trouble controlling the dramatic emotions of the pink. He or she would need to reach into his or her depth to bring the blue into action so that its revelations can calm the pink. It is, Of course, possible to achieve. Both qualities at once then become purplish.

If it is working as an integrated energy field, using all the available potentials, then a purplish mixture or glow is seen near the blue and pink, even though the essence of the ray itself does not change, it is still blue and pink. It works together in harmony. And you see this reflected in the aura as this integrated activity radiates forth. The two qualities are then working in unison with balanced or equal power, another mode in which a rainmaker is one to raise an equal weight. When each color expresses 50 percent of the current, it is called the dual rate in counseling sessions with a dual rate person. I often say to them as we begin, you're very indecisive, aren't you? And they look at me in astonishment.

I say, you've got poor circulation, too. They agree and ask how I know this. I will explain. You've got to do all right, 50 percent of one and 50 percent of the other. And you never know exactly which two bucks you're going to use. It's like having a carpenter's tool box and a plumber's tool box, each containing a hammer that looks a little bit different from the other. Do all right, people are constantly wondering which tool to use, so they play a cosmic ping pong, should I or shouldn't I? Many people with dual races seem to be born with their sunshine in Libra or Gemini. That is the only correlation I've ever seen between sunshines and. Needless to say, not every Doray person is a Gemini or a Libra. One more type of raid to consider is the multiple raid, which is seen relatively rarely. It might be made up of three colors, for example, divided into 40 percent and 40 percent and 20 percent.

Chapter - 18

The three different raids are occurring at once, one of the seven principal is a multiple raid made up of three different colors, and there is another and that is a two color day in the following analysis. These are the first and second raids, respectively. The seven raise. Let us now take a look at the seven races, the order in which they are given here does not denote a hierarchy of importance or a sequence that is followed in any way. It is simply my system of organizing the different qualities that correlate with the colors in the incoming energy current. In my classes, students are asked to determine which of the seven raises their rate; they're frequently able to guess correctly simply by considering the characteristics of each.

Of course, it is not possible for me to validate your choice visually, as I would do in class. However, if you practice the exercises given in Chapter four, you should be able to confirm the color of your array with your own vision. There is nothing miraculous about seeing the race. It simply takes practice. In attempting to understand the race, it is helpful to realize that they represent various combinations of the primary qualities in human nature. Everyone has all these qualities in varying degrees, but each of us has a unique mixture with different emphases on the various aspects. As I perceive and understand it, the role of each individual is the main current of energy entering from the universe into the human being.

As I mentioned in Chapter one, the chakras are dynamic, distributing centers of the right. We might say that this is the main power line from the central power station, the universe, and that the chakras are absolutely distribution centers on the main power line. First rate, electric, blue, white, vermilion, red qualities, power, will, courage, leadership, self-reliance. The three colors of this race can be in harmony, but frequently one color is emphasized and the potential balance is lost. Walking the path of this right is like walking a razor's edge. It takes great concentration and balance to handle its power. We can more readily understand the origin of the power in the first day if we examine its underlying principle.

The three rings in one are actually a trinity in Christian symbols, and it is a covenant of the Father, Son and Holy Ghost in our own beings. The Trinity is the soul, the mind and the body. We can see these three aspects in the seven chakras correlating with the penile pituitary and thyroid centers, the red very signifies the creator God WhiteWave reflects the totality of the Goodhead and it's the Christ consciousness. This is the expression or manifestation of creative energy. An individual working on the first row must bring all these qualities at once. And that is why this path is one of the most difficult. It is also quite rare. If you could look into these people's lives, you would see that they are constantly in turmoil within themselves, they have difficulty choosing their direction.

Their main characteristics are courage, willpower and self-reliance. But when the quality of power overwhelms the other aspects they seek to conquer, this defeats their purpose of expressing the Trinity because God does not need to fight or conquer. Actually, we can say that the goal of the first is to merge with an individual's will, with God's will, to transmute the human ego with the divine ego and then express it. It takes courage to allow the two to combine because it means that the individual must face the unknown. The only place where the divine will can be found is within the seat of your own consciousness.

It takes a lot of courage to enter the unknown realms of the inner self, too many people stand in front of the mirror and see only their personal identities rather than the unknown divine inner self. They can perceive only the outer shell, it takes courage to drop the shell and look deep inside. This is the greatest struggle for first rate people because they have power in the world. They're often the last to turn their eyes inward and find even greater powers there, although they exercise a strict discipline over the physical and mental realms and over other people for sure. People often lack courage when it comes to the challenges of the spiritual realm.

However, when the individual having the red, white and blue rays choose an integration of these three qualities, he or she becomes a leader in the highest sense of the word by providing others with a model of behavior. There is then no power or Congress involved, rather, the energy flows through him or her and becomes a continuum of aid flowing and flowing like. People with this right can collect enormous energy and then express it and thus create an exemplary model of self-reliance for others to observe. However, in order to be self-reliant, one needs to sacrifice the self to the self by understanding that the self is an expression of the entire cosmos, that it is complete in itself and does not need to seek its completion externally.

In medieval times, for sure, people often became alchemist's transmuting energy into its manifest form as power. First rate people can also become pioneers or great statesmen or even dictators. Unless their power has a spiritual goal, it can drive them to seek victory over the world. Hitler was on the first rate, as I have confirmed from personal observation of the Fuhrer during World War Two. He uses power in a negative way because he was fixated on material goals. Using the capability of the first rate to transfer or hypnotize people, Hitler was able to lead them into action that they would not have committed under their own wills.

There are many examples of dictator types who could fascinate others into following them, although we have no actual visual proof of the fact Rasputin and Napoleon also exemplify the first type who is functioning on willpower that is directed by unconscious motivations without the higher spiritual guidance that would bring purity to their actions. First, three people can become confused by their power and try to make everyone else subordinate to themselves. In fact, their only true satisfaction will come from finding the ultimate reality of themselves. Their powers should be used for this quest alone. But if you have the courage to face this enormous goal, instead they choose the easier way and express their energy and physical domination.

In relationships, first rate, people behave in a distinctive manner. They guide and direct and are quite charismatic with little softness in their manner. When they say no, they mean it, though they may have a certain kind of grin on their faces. They know that we often hurt what we love. There's a saying that gentle doctors make ugly wounds. The first person is not a gentle doctor when he guides, he's a rough surgeon who puts a knife to you and cuts. After you believe he collects the blood and pours it back into you. First day people are at their best under adversity. It is then that they can test their power and leadership. When everything runs smoothly, there's nothing to challenge them. They like to tackle a tough problem and solve it quickly by taking actions that others may not even understand.

They can be like piledriver drivers using their enormous power to overcome difficulties or to convert you to their beliefs. Ultimately, they can transcend this forcefulness and become examples of their beliefs rather than dictators. Avoid a first rate person, teachers, by saying to the students, don't come to me anymore. I have learned by doing so. If you would follow my example. Stop asking me what to do, you know, already. So begin to act. But only those who have learned to integrate the three rays and all their qualities can achieve this ideal, the highest attainment of the first individual is to move beyond human laws and social restraints and themselves to become the law.

Then divine will and their personal will become one. When this occurs, they can display amazing abilities, their power over physical reality allows them to materialize and dematerialize. They have domination over nature because they use the laws of nature effortlessly to fulfill their high schools. Although such abilities were demonstrated by great masters such as Christ, the concept of Christ consciousness goes beyond the first raised potentials and no longer needed the power of the first wave because his spiritual awareness was so expanded that he could use another tool to fulfill his purpose. The method of non resistance, which in the new age to come, will replace the present attitude of an eye for an eye, a tooth for a tooth.

Christ worked on the pure white race. He was not involved with any of the colors anymore. As first rate people struggle to integrate the trinity of qualities and achieve balance, they are vulnerable to certain weaknesses. These include tyranny, pride, domination, thirst for power and rigidity. Regionally the mind often makes the body rigid, so frustrated people often suffer from arthritis. Try to change their mind and you are sure to fail. When they experience defeat, degradation and displacement, they are easily humiliated. Despite these problems, first rays have a wonderful destiny to fulfill when they achieve harmonious interaction among the three aspects of their beings, they embody the connection between the macrocosm and the macrocosm.

They personify the law of correspondences as above, so below. When this powerful rate is integrated by the attainment of a highly spiritual awareness, it no longer appears as three distinct colors. It becomes the one flowing to a soft lavender orchid color. This can lead to confusion when you're observing someone whom you formerly observed to be on the first day when the three colors blend, the individual now suddenly appears to be on the seventh rate, which is purple. However, this temporary state of affairs occurs only rarely, and the three colors are really there, although they're blended and appear for the moment to be one. Second rate as your blue and golden yellow qualities, universal love, wisdom, insight, intuition.

This is the only two color gray among the seven races, basically, it can be called the messenger. The blue signifies the ability to give form and so it manifests the content of the gold in yellow, which is wisdom. Secondly, many people who emphasize the golden yellow tend to be clairvoyants and are especially sensitive to conscious sources of information. If they utilize the blue more than the gold, they become teachers, religious reformers or healers. The qualities of the second are love and wisdom. Wisdom is a knowledge gained when you experience something through your mind, body and soul, then you are the knowledge. It is much more than an intellectual knowing it is knowing something by being it, doing it and living it.

For example, how can one know love? We can only know what we already are if we look within our natures, it is clear that we are part of the whole universe, children of God or expressions of the divine spark. As this realization dawns, it is accompanied by a feeling of the love of God, people cannot have love unless it is through the love of the divine. It is that simple. We start with the source at all times, and we cannot obtain the love of humanity simply through the love for our fellow humans, we have to obtain it through the source, through the divine love that we carry within us, that we, in fact, are. Love and wisdom are born together.

That's the Greek word philos and Sophia combined together to give us philosophy when there is love, there's also understanding that can embrace both the positive and the negative qualities of the loved one. When I hear someone say I love him or her, but I do not understand him or her, I recognize that is a man made love, not God, love for one, would not separate the good and bad aspects of a person's being if he or she realized that that individuals endowed with the totality of divinity and is expressing that God within to the best of his or her ability. By experiencing the divine within ourselves, we're able to love others wholly. Thus, the path to inner knowing that is wisdom is also the way to truth loving.

The golden and Blu-ray identifies the messengers of this universal love. These people do not care if they gain recognition or appreciation from others because they recognize the God within themselves. They follow an individual journey guided by the insights from their open channel to the conscious mind. They combine universal love with the ability to express that love, and thus they are deeply compassionate. Empathy, not sympathy, is their attitude towards others. They take action and help to relieve the suffering in the world because they feel no separation from the rest of humanity.

The second right sees you as him or herself without judging your condition. He or she tries to alleviate your difficulties.

The motivating impulses of second rate people are to say, to teach and to share love and wisdom, their messengers who will go through a fire to fulfill these impulses. In its highest expression, people on the right are entirely selfless, not attached and fully aware of the unity of all life. They say you're me and I'm you and your philosophy, your profession that strives toward a realization of the whole human potential of giving flesh to the world partakes of the qualities of the second ray. For example, doctors who treat the mind, body and soul as an integral system are practicing New Age medicine under the auspices of the gold and blue ray.

Using the capabilities of the second rate, individuals can act in ways that benefit everyone in a way they are Maziar's meaning messengers who bring light and the message of an unlimited universal love. This is the maximum development of the second rate, however, it takes much trial and error in the left to accomplish perfect expression, as is true for people of all categories of race. If an individual does not realize his or her purpose, his or her life is a meaningless puzzle. If a second person does not put into action what he or she knows intuitively, thereby validating it, he or she becomes dull and resentful. Stagnant pools become cesspools. Rather than loving the second rate, people can carry the most hatred and bitterness of all the races. In such cases, they actually hate themselves because they do not understand themselves.

Chapter - 19

And sadly, they've been like everyone else in the world. Even those who have awakened to their potential suffer when they are unable to express themselves perfectly. Sentimentality and attachment rather than love, then emerging sensuality and passion take precedence over compassion. Such people are impractical and sometimes make impulsive, unwise decisions. You could say they have their heads in the clouds, but are unable to bring what they see down to earth, they assume that abstractions and ideas are higher than the concrete earth based expressions of things. Isolated in their own manifested visions, individuals on the second ranking suffer from loneliness, often their hearts are broken because they feel alienated and misunderstood by others.

Such individuals withdraw until they're martyrs at that point, the most help someone can give them is to scold them for their self pity. They need other people for their creativity is expressed only when they can bring their wisdom into the world. When individuals on the second they express their imbalances in disease, they are prone to mental disorders, skin ailments and dysfunctions of the liver and the pineal gland. Third-rate, emerald green qualities, comprehension, mental power, adaptability, tact, impartiality. The color green finds its origin in the blending of two primary colors, blue and yellow. This is not to be confused with the second rate, which is blue and gold, and which consists of two separate, distinct colors. Who symbolizes willpower and volition and yellow is the color of intellect.

Right, people give form to many creative ideas that they see in the consciousness of others. However, they're only planters and do not stay to garden and watch the seed grow into a fruit bearing plant. Using their excellent ability to evaluate, they choose fertile fields and know just what is needed for certain plants to grow. I'm using this analogy with plans for the particular reason that green made persons are the greatest lovers of nature. They feel most at home in a green natural environment. Of course, they avoid crowds and seem aloof at times when they enter a room, they have a cooling effect, unlike a first rate person who activates and thus heats the atmosphere.

The main potentials within the green person are creative innovation and inventiveness. Wherever people are sources of ideas, they rarely implement them. Rather, they provide impetus for the creativity of others, encouraging personal growth and the perception of the divine nature of all people. People on the third rate excel as healers of the body, mind and spirit. They're impartial judges who love truth and quickly discern what is false, logical, reasonable and practical, Greenway's can build powerful intellect. Many great scholars, philosophers and authors are on the third way. They are extremely critical, but their criticism is mostly constructive and non-punitive.

In fact, some third rate people will withhold criticism for fear of hurting others. Because of their receptivity and love of perfection, these people have difficulty in allowing the seeds they sell to develop as they will not all seeds will grow if the green person stays and watches the seeds, his or her own growth stops and he or she may even suffocate the seed. The Chapter to be learned here is to become non attached to creative efforts to let them go and create more. Often the third individual tends to be a perfectionist, fear of acting in an imperfect way then makes the individual indecisive. Misery cannot bear to make mistakes or suffer any indignity.

He or she may be quite cunning in order to avoid these discomforts. There is also a possibility of becoming too judgmental and critical of oneself and of others. Most of the greenery people I've observed are quite introverted, they generally prefer to write what they feel and think about it rather than to speak about it. Green rays are most susceptible to malfunctions of the kidneys and the pituitary gland, they may suffer from hypothyroidism, water retention, consumption and poor circulation. Forthright, Tony, bronze, orange qualities, stability, harmony, rhythm, beauty balance. The Tony bronze orange color of the fourth ring is derived from a mixture of red, the color of energy and vitality, yellow, the color of intellect and green, the color of growth.

The red and yellow, plenty of orange, the color of intuition, the more orange, the red, the more intuitive the person is. However, it is only when there is also a blending of some green to give the race a tiny bronze hue that a practical element is added to the intuitive. More than any other time, the fourth ray wants to create harmony. To sum it up in one word, these people are catalysts. They have a clear, intuitive knowledge of the tools in their tool kit, and they use them to find the beauty they love in others and in the world. Some become cosmic sponges, physically absorbing everything around them, whether it is positive or negative. They like to be in the middle of everything, even to the point of meddling in other people's problems.

Usually they have a beneficial effect and are capable of bringing peace where there is a battle of opposites occurring. That is why I envision them as being like the fulcrum of whatever they do not empower or enlighten, but they provide the ballast necessary for the other ways to act effectively. The fourth person rescued others from extremes and imbalances. People tend to confide in these orange individuals who often carry the burden of others problems. This story is particularly connected with the energy of the heart chakra until individuals attain a perfected expression of this energy. They may be quite flighty and indiscriminate about love.

Sometimes they become so eager to fulfill their race that they try to bring harmony everywhere, they are then inconsistent in their emotions and rather unreliable and impractical. Orangery people are also jack, of all trades, but master of none. They have to act on the impulse of the moment and specialization would demand too much concentration from them. Their ideas and interests vacillate from moment to moment. They need variety and would become bored if they were to continue at one speciality. They need to express themselves in beautiful ways and so do many artists.

Because their purpose makes them quite reliant on the attention of others. They tend to over dramatize and inflate emotions and situations beyond the actual facts. When they cannot play their catalytic role, they become moody and extremely depressed. This is a difficult day to live, even though imbues individuals with a glow of charisma, they often fall prey to self-indulgence and conceit. At times, they will use any method to attract the attention and involvement of other people so that they can play a controlling role in life. Orangery people seeking their own balance in order to be perfect harmonizers of others are prone to certain physical problems, including a tendency to obesity, water retention and other hypothyroidism or hypothyroidism.

Fifth, Ray Lemon yellow. Qualities, logic, accuracy, tolerance, patience. This is a very intellectual function in its purest expression, individuals with a yellow rate love facts. Their motivation in life is to find out the answer to every question, to verify their knowledge through logic. Although their vision is narrow, the single focus helps them pierce the shadows of ignorance and discover new information. They can offer clear explanations of things, and their manner of presentation is rather dry because they fear that expressing emotion will get in the way of facts and figures. Ancillary people have extreme difficulty in relaxing and relating to others in a spontaneous way.

They are very serious and solemn or objective about their ideas and stimulate people with excitement about their ideas. These are the people who know every word of the law and uphold it rigidly. Because of their tunnel vision, they're frequently unable to see the whole picture to understand how the facts fit together. Yet they love chess or puzzles because of the intellectual challenge and the lack of emotional involvement. More materialistic than any other race cannot stand criticism and are rarely involved in a quest for self-knowledge. They make excellent researchers and lawyers. In the arts, they're mainly interested in form and accuracy rather than inspiration.

There people have provided the world with precise information about our physical universe, they develop and implement the faculty of conscious, rational thought until it is razor-sharp. Because of this focus on their life purpose, they tend to suffer from inflexibility of mind and body. There may be physical problems such as migraine headaches, muscle spasms and arthritis. Meditation and relaxation methods, combined with visualization exercises, may help them to discover other aspects of their beings and become less rigid. It is relatively rare to find a person with a pure yellow ray. Most have subways, and so the moderating influence of the subway can be brought out through appropriate disciplines.

Fixed rate, Rosebank. Qualities one point in this devotion, sacrificial love, loyalty. The Pingrup produces evangelical people, they serve others in doing so, they're actually serving themselves and fulfilling their primary goal of teaching people to raise their consciousness. The sixth person seeks to help everyone realize the angelic nature within themselves. They always have a cause to which they're totally devoted. Because they feel that they are particularly in tune with the cosmic order, they can be intolerant of the advice of others and resentful if they're misunderstood.

People on the street are capable of sacrificing their lower egos to their humanitarian goals, their romantic, emotional and sentimental annual martyred themselves for love of their cause. They can give themselves totally and are the most loyal of all the raise, this is because they understand inwardly that if they are true to themselves, they're automatically true to others. When the red component of the pinger is dominant, these people can be fiery evangelists whose enthusiasm can lead to martyrdom. Such a lack of balance makes them Massachusetts and thus less effective in fulfilling their mission of love. Six or eight people may try to teach in too soft a manner.

There is one word in the dictionary that they do not know, and that is no. They hum and haw, and the best they can say is, well, no, but perhaps. Gullible, tender and hesitant, angry people are somewhat unsure of themselves if they must hurt you a little to heal or teach you. They cannot withstand adversity and always attempt to flow and love and harmony with others. When these motivations and tendencies are expressed in extremes of self-sacrifice and martyrdom, angry people will suffer from various kinds of abdominal problems. Seven, three purple. Qualities, precision, grace, dignity, nobility, activity, integration, ritualism, designing, synthesizing.

The Purple Rain is a blending of red, white and blue, red, as mentioned previously, represents the activation of available energies that is power and vitality. Lou represents direction, giving powers or willpower, quite a blending of all colors represents purity, truth, the all encompassing expression of the universal source. When these colors are blended, purple results the exact year, depending on the proportion of the colors. The more white there is, the more awkward the race will be, the more red, the deeper purple, the more blue, the darker violet. The red, white and blue of the first are not intrusively blended.

However, when a first rate person integrates for brief periods the results in people who may be temporarily mistaken for a purple rain. Individuals who have the purple right are distinguished by their noble bearing, although they're not necessarily considered, they are misunderstood because of their regal appearance. They love ceremony and ritual and power. Many become interested in magic and have strong psychic sensitivities. However, unless they're well balanced in their own identities, they can be superstitious and victimized by lower forms of practice's. Popery people are like the sun. They need a lot of freedom to act and express themselves.

If others get too close, they may be disintegrated by this powerful rain, yet others are strongly attracted to the sun. When the sun does not respond in kind, there are difficulties in mutual understanding, purple people are frequently insecure because they're so often isolated by their acquaintances. Another expression of the dignified quality of purple rain is a love of symmetry and formality. They grasp things as a whole and are not interested in the details of the picture. During that, they know more than others who would rather do it themselves and are quite self-sufficient.

This still keeps them out of reach of many people, and they are thus slow to form relationships.

Purple Rain works that provide them with the opportunity to give graceful form to their holistic ideas such as the arts, interior design or fashion design. All right, people are motivated to maintain a noble, ceremonious and orderly existence. Because the world in which they live is often chaotic and crude, people in the seventh race suffer from imbalances primarily through nervous tension and disorders of the adrenal glands. Working with the ray. In determining your own race, there are a few considerations to keep in mind. First, remember that the seven rays represent qualities that are within everyone. You're right, is the particular quality that you want to learn most about in this lifetime.

At first, therefore, you may actually express some of the other ways better than your own, if you had already mastered your array, there would be no need for you to experience it now. Unless you're quite keen that you know the color of your right, it is best that you keep all of them in mind. As you become familiar with the qualities they embody, it will be easier to assign the rate to yourself or to others. Ultimately, by following the exercises described in Chapter four, you should be able to see the race directly rather than infer them. Many people do not exhibit one or the other of the seven principle races. Instead, they have a combination of two or more of the seven races. When such combinations are clearly defined, it is possible to understand the significance of these people's rise by noting the location and proportions of the various colors.

Finally, I want to caution you about observing the way or the aura. Remember that you are looking through your own aura when you leave someone else. This is why self-knowledge is so essential for anyone engaging in any type of physical, emotional or spiritual therapy or counseling. You must be able to distinguish your own qualities and problems from those of the people you are trying to help. No one is or perfectly self aware. Furthermore, there may be many phenomena vibrating below or above your perceptual capacity. When I speak with a student or a client, I always suggest that he or she take my word with a grain of salt. Each person is his or her own best judge of what is applicable to his or her own life. If you can give the fruits of your vision to others and encourage them to keep what is valuable and throw out the rest, then you have truly been of service to them.

Chapter - 20

Three to seven Auric Fields. If the right is the input or the current, then the Ora is the output or ammunition. Whereas the ratios what your potentials are, the orishas, what you're experiencing and what you have experienced by understanding the patterns of the aura and mapping it out in each individual case, it is possible to make a prognosis of what a person might experience in the future if he or she uses the energy that we know are available as shown by the ray. Everything that I will be saying about the aura has come to me in an empirical way that is through direct personal experience. Although I began to see these human energy fields at a very young age, I did not understand what I was seeing until much later. Over thirty five years of observation, I have noticed that people have certain things in common, similar diseases, mental states, behavior patterns when their auras look a certain way.

In nineteen seventy one, for example, I was asked by a doctor in Vancouver, British Columbia, with whom I frequently consult to take a look at a twenty eight year old patient with. On observing this patient, I was able to report that he had tuberculosis in April nineteen sixty three, followed by a collapsed lung, all of which the doctor was able to confirm from the patient's records. I observed something else in the patient that I had never seen before. I remarked to the doctor, a very interesting thing is happening in the bloodstream, it says, If I see a little steel fillings looking like tiny silver fish that are apparently attacking another smaller and darker particle and after it attacks it, it sort of devours it every time that happens, I see a little ripples coming out as soon as it has been devoured. I don't know what this is.

It turned out that the patient was a heroin addict and that the doctor had just placed him on methadone. The doctor suggested that what I was seeing was probably the action of the methadone on the heroin. About three or four months later, a young man came into my counseling room and I saw the same thing occurring in his blood. I immediately asked him, how long have you been on methadone? He was rather surprised, to say the least. That is the empirical way I've learned to map out the human energy field by seeing the same occurrence in different situations in different individuals. I'm sure the mapping is not complete yet. Every day I see new things for which I do not yet have an answer.

There is still a great deal to be learned about the meanings of the patterns and the aura, but I will relate some of what I have been able to learn so far. The human atmosphere or aura surrounds you in every direction, although it is represented in drawings as two dimensional, always bear in mind that it is three dimensional. This energy field is made up of vortices that move in different directions and together make up an elliptical or egg like shape. Those who have read the books of Caspian Derrida or the writings of some of the series will recognize this description of an egg shaped energy field. They're horizontal, as well as vertical energy fields made up of vortices within vortices, within vortices.

The human arm is made up of different levels of density as we move away from the human body, the energy fields become progressively subtler and more difficult to see. Because of this, we know considerably more about the aura closer to the body than we do about some of the subtlest ones. We have all had the experience of observing such an energy field made up of varying layers of density, although we may not have realized it. In the familiar experience of looking at a candle flame, one can discern different levels of density as represented by different colors and degrees of subtlety. Right around the work, you will see a bluish form surrounded by a dark area that is also bluish gray. Then there's an oval shape of a golden or yellowish color.

And within that yellowish , you can make out layers of varying degrees of subtlety beyond the flame itself. You can see. So we're all shaped fields of energy, a sort of dissipation glow. The human aura, like the Campbell Flame, is made of progressively subtle levels of density. Let us begin by looking at the one closest to the body. The physical aura. A number of recent books have stated that the aura has been photographed, this is not exactly true. Through the use of the techniques of Careline photography, a small part of the total aura has been photographed, perhaps a fraction of an inch.

Total Aurum may extend as far as 15 or 20 feet, but on the average, a normal active person will have an hour, five to eight feet in diameter. What then has been photographed? If you look alongside the physical body right next to the skin, you may see an ammunition of light coming out, which is called the Corona. But between the corona and the skin, there appears to be a space which we call the band about one eighth inch wide. This man has been photographed entirely in photography in more technical terms. The man is called the Galvanic Skin Resistance. The ban has no color and looks like a dark green gap or a very narrow black hole. It is neither an ammunition nor an absorption.

It is more like a temporary resistance to outflow. This band can be seen in the killing photog. RAF, because these photographs are made by passing a high voltage electric current through the object being photographed. There is no other source of light, the bed then represents the resistance to the outflow of this current. Surrounding the span of resistance, we have the first Korona of ammunition. This part, which looks like a shadow form of your physical structure, is sometimes referred to in esoteric literature as an etheric body. In the tradition, no classification of elements, earth, water, fire and air philosophers call the subtler substance that fills the void between these elements.

Arthur. This concept in more modern times is once again becoming popular among scientists. It is true that this, the densest of all the human energy fields, should be called the etheric body. I feel rather that the more subtle should be called a Ferrick, and I prefer to call this the physical aura. This is the area most closely related to the physiology of the body and is the one that is used to diagnose physical disturbances. Of course, these disturbances can be seen in the other airflows as well, because all the ammunition are a result of the totality, but definite physiological disturbances are read in the physical or.

In the healthy person, the physical area extends from four inches to about eight or rarely 12 inches from the body. Under normal, healthy circumstances, it is a smoky blue color, like a smoke screen around the body because it is closest to the body, the physical aura is apparently closely related to the infrared frequencies or the frequencies of heat. Some people have claimed to see a foggy glow around the person, the first Apollo astronauts who landed on the moon was pictured in photographs as having a blue glow around him. At least one reporter said that this glove represented the discovery of a strange energy fuel. Of course, that strange energy was there even when he was on the earth, but the airless surface of the moon made it possible for it to become visible on camera.

The physical area is not very bright. This is in contrast with Careline photography, which shows it to be brilliant and colorful. What makes a corona so bright in the killing photograph is that there is a Tesla coil or Vandergriff generator connected to the instrument by which the picture was taken that generates an electrostatic field higher in voltage than the energy outside that field. The electrostatic field filters out all electrical noises and disturbances, thereby insulating the object being filmed within it. So it is therefore logical that there is a greater capacity to make an image on the photographic plate and that the image will look brighter.

Surrounding the smoking blue corona that some people call it, their body is an energy field shaped like an egg or an oval that I called over the oven that stands about a foot or a foot and a half to two feet away from the body. It is still part of the physical aura, it is the dissipating outflow of the corona which becomes progressively settled the farther away it is from the body. In most cases, the owner is of a dirty golden or ivory white color. Most people who say they have seen it as if they were not actually seeing the rate have seen either the corona of the physical aura or the golden eye over people around them. Because this is still part of the densest of the energy fields, it is more readily visible.

In the physical aura, then we have first the band, then the Corona, which also has been called the physical aura or the body and then the open. The human body, surrounded by the ovum and the physical aura, resembles an egg yolk and what surrounds the egg white is the other energy fields around it. You float within the energy fuels that we are creating and with which we are making contact with the universe again in our subtle ammunition. The ovum resembles an egg flattened on one end, like the legendary egg of Columbus. Columbus gave his men a riddle while aboard his ship, he told them that he could make it stand on end.

Of course, they said he could not do it, but the egg would fall over. Columbus hard boiled an egg and pushed it down and it stood up. The flat end of your physical area shows that you're integrally connected through your energies with the soil, your energies are influenced by what radiates from the soil, and at the same time, you're influencing the soil you walk on. If we could amplify the energies coming out of the body, we would see that it is made up of vortices of energy. If an organ starts to malfunction, there's not enough energy activity in it, and instead of radiating outward, it starts to absorb energy. One such absorption takes place, the ammunition in the corresponding part of the physical art begins to look dull, less blue and more silver.

Great. And the more it absorbs the darker variable look, until eventually it will look like a black hole or an empty space, when it is black, it represents a grave situation anywhere. A dark spot occurs. And the physical aura, you know, that is where a physiological disturbance is taking place. And someone who observes the aura may see such a physiological disturbance occurring even before the person's aware of any feedback from it. Similarly, if an organ or system becomes excessive in its action, we see a very bright spot around that area, for example, and hypothyroidism, you would see a very bright light around the throat area.

Lately, we have seen tremendously bright light around the pituitary and penile area and around the solar plexus adrenal system in young children who have been diagnosed as hyperkinetic or hyperactive. Unfortunately, some children are treated with drugs that suppress their high energy level rather than being directed to be quiet. These children should be helped to use their high energy in functional ways. It is not good to have the high energy stay around the solar plexus and around the pituitary and pineal gland. The whole body should be equally radiant and the extra brightness in these areas show that there is an imbalance in the system. By creatively stabilizing this energy, the child can deal with this high energy input.

Besides observing its brightness, we can also get information from the extension of the physical aura if a person has several organs malfunctioning so that these organs are not radiating but absorbing energy, the size of the physical aura will become narrower, denser, more opaque, because now it gives off less radiance. It does not expand so far anymore because the frequency becomes higher and the amplitude lower and consequently the wavelength shorter. If the body starts to become deceased and more absorption than radiation takes place, the ovum contract becomes denser and the color is denser and more opaque, not so golden ivory as it was.

So if you saw nothing but this contraction and denseness, you would know that there is something wrong in the physical system, even though you had not yet determined exactly where the physical system is malfunctioning. The emotional aura. The next demolition I call the emotional aura, the emotional aura begins at the outer edge of the ovum, about one and a half feet from the body. It varies greatly in a way, but on the average, it reaches out about another eight to 12 inches. Some esoteric people have called it the astral aura astral meaning from the stars. It is true that this particular energy field would be stimulated by cosmic influences such as the stars, but it is also influenced by other factors, such as a person who may be affecting your emotions that would immediately cause the emotional area to change.

The planets and the stars do have a great influence on our emotional nature. Well, let us not forget the Chapter learned in voluntary controls that every mental and emotional occurrence is also a physiological occurrence. And so it affects the radiant admonition from the physical body. The emotional aura is one of the most difficult of the energy fields around the body. Sometimes I've seen as many as sixty four colors occurring at once in the emotional aura. This is because there's a lot of activity going on and emotions all the time. The emotions are much smaller than the physical substance, and sometimes they run ahead of the physical substance.

In the emotional aura, a multitude of different changes are constantly taking place because even if we do not realize it, we're a. bombarded by external as well as internal stimuli, which in turn produce chemical changes. The secretion of hormones, for example, is based on emotional stimuli, every thought immediately creates an emotional response because emotion is energy, emotion.

Chapter - 21

The more energy that is being activated, the more reflection that takes place in the colors of the emotional aura when the colors are excessive. We say that the person is super emotional or hyper emotional, and then the emotional state starts to have backlashes on the physical body. Under normal circumstances, all the colors of the spectrum may be seen in the emotional aura, where do these colors come from? Changes take place in your physical structure. An increased or decreased state of functioning, which constitutes a transition in your physical structure, will have an effect on the chakra or dynamo that resonates with the outer world as well as with the inner world.

This effect on the choker will then influence the energy that you radiate, the emotional aura will show a specific color related to the specific chakra that is affected more than the others. Of course, all the choppers interact and do not readily function separately, but according to the color that is seen, an emotional aura is located in relation to the seven chakras. It is possible to tell how a certain kind of energy is being used in the organism. The emotional aura, then, is a relatively explicit radiation indicating the action of the choppers. Of course, the colors of the choppers themselves are continually changing, just as the colors and the emotions are constantly shifting. But the base colors of the chakras rarely change, if at all.

Table to review the best colors of the chakras and what kinds of energies they represent. Table to base colors of the chopra's chakra, root color, red or orange type of energy like promoting energy, vital physical energy, chakra spleen. Color, pink type of energy, love, reserve energy. Chakra, solar plexus, color, green type of energy growth and healing left reserving energy chakra part. Color, golden, yellow, gold type of energy, consciousness, mental energy. Chakra throat. Color blue. Type of energy volition, expressive energy. Chakra Rao. Color, indigo type of energy, transitional color, synthesizing energy. Chakra crown.

Color, pale, purple orchid type of energy integration. As the table indicates, the base color of the root chakra, which is associated with the gonads, is red orange. This is the color of vital physical energy, as we shall see, when this vital energy moves up through the chakras and is expressed at a higher level, it undergoes changes that are reflected in the colors, evident in the emotional aura. The peak of the spring chakra is the color of love, the spleen also functions as a reserve battery for the body and also represents reserve energy. When I observe bright, clear energy fields around a person, and if my own aura is also clear and bright, the other person's body becomes translucent to my vision.

Because the person is in my aura, it is as if the molecules of the body are displaced. In such cases, it is possible to see a pinkish glow around the entire nervous system if the body becomes even more translucent, we may also see the meridians of acupuncture, which are also pinkish in color. Miss Pink, which is associated with the subtle anatomic systems of the body, is the pink of reserve or low energy. The best color of the solar plexus is chakra green, which is the color of life preserving energy. This is the stabilizing there as the vital energy moves up from the rooftop with through the emotional plane of the solar plexus, it is preserved by being cooled down in preparation for moving into the next state, the rational and the conscious state of the heart chakra. The heart chakra is associated with golden yellow or gold, which is the energy of consciousness of mental energy.

We have seen that energy undergoes transformations in the Book of moving through the chakras and that the heart chakra is the set of the transmutation of fire into light as we move upward or light into fire as we move downward. As energy is passed through the crucible of the heart chakra, they undergo transformations that are reflected in a change of color at this chakra, the blue of the thyroid chakra is the color of willpower of volition of expressive energy. The chakra has a base color of indigo, which is actually a transitional color comprising the three primary colors in the process of mixing and blending. The energy represented by this transitional color is synthesizing energy and the pituitary gland associated with this chakra is not surprisingly called the master gland because it synthesizes the hormones that regulate the entire endocrine system of the body.

The purpose of the crown chakra is made up of the two primary colors, red and blue, combined with white, which contains all colors. This purple violet color is the color of integration. This chakra associated with the pineal gland represents the integration of positive and negative of creation and destruction of absorption and radiation. Energy in the form of light is absorbed by the pineal gland as energy moves down through the chakras. We've seen that it has transformed from light, fire to substance as it moves back up. It is once again transmuted from substance to fire to light. When the individual is functioning in a truly integrated manner, the violet of the crown chakra shows that the functioning of the organs and chakras is nicely balanced and blended and that there's a continuous input and outflow of energy.

The input, Of course, represented, by the way, and the output by the aura. Once we know what qualities are represented by the colors of various chakras, we can tell what an individual is emotionally by interpreting the colors we see according to the types of energies they represent and where these colors are located. The colors in the emotional aura have a definite relationship to the base colors of the chakras. In all the years I've been observing the energy fields around people, I've never seen, for example, the right vermilion bed of the root chakra occurring anywhere above the solar plexus and the emotional aura. I've also seen it below the solar plexus. I've seen the red orange emerging with other colors above the solar plexus, but then it becomes pink or orange or purple, violet or indigo, but it never has the solid red orange of the base color.

If you see red orange around the shoulders, there is something wrong with your observation. You're missing the color the red orange is merging with. This is a useful principle to keep in mind a good test of the accuracy of your observation. In a healthy state, the colors and the aura are not identical to the colors of the corresponding chakras, for example, because the base color of the solar plexus checks with green, you might assume that if you see green around the solar plexus, it means everything is fine. But that is not so. It means that the chakra is not very active. If it is active, the colors will be in a continuous state of transformation, green is only the base color.

The more active the chakra, the smaller the base, color or axis. If the solar plexus remained green, nothing from above could come below and nothing from below could come about. If a person has a green band only around the solar plexus area, you would say that the person was in a state of growth but was not permitting the growth to develop up from the soil that he or she was not letting it go. Just as the red orange is never seen above the solar plexus area, the purple of the crown chakra is very rarely seen below or at the level of the solar plexus. We see down to the solar plexus area, but very rarely have I seen it below the solar plexus. It cannot go through the heart chakra and come out the same color in the solar plexus area below.

As soon as the subtle color of purple begins to affect the heart dynamo, we see it merging into a brown bronze bronzer, more orange color. We're dealing with different types of forces that can intermix what then do not retain their characteristic colors anymore. If you see purple in the solar plexus area, either you're seeing wrong or you're seeing an internal state between the lower energies or red, orange and pink and the energies in the solar plexus area. This means that the person is emotionally integral with his own system as well as with the outside world. When you meditate, according to the methods outlined in voluntary controls, there are visible changes in the emotional aura when you chant the second purple begins to appear around the solar plexus area. This represents a stabilization and integration of the upper functions with the lower.

The lower energy starts to pump up to the heart area and the upper starts to pump down. Similarly, if I take the green of the solar plexus and bring it up and out through the heart chakra, it will not be the same green anymore. It will now be a yellowish green or charged rose because now gold has been added to it from the heart chakra. All the colors you see above the heart chakra should have a golden sheen to them. The only place in the emotional aura where it is healthy to see an increase in the original base color is in the heart chakra. There we see the golden orange becoming brighter and brighter with the greater activity. The heart chakra is the alchemist's vessel, the cauldron in which the transmutation from fire into light and from light into fire takes place.

The more that is released from below and the more that comes from above, the more activity occurs and the radiation of the gold light and the consciousness is concomitant. We expanded. The energy is so alive then that there is an arousal of consciousness that also affects the physical body, you may feel a sensation of tightness in the chest area. The mental aura, the other arms are not so complicated as the emotional aura, the next one, the mental aura, is a narrower band than the emotional. The emotional aura starts about one and a half feet away from the body and reaches out perhaps to within eight to 12 inches. The mental hour extends about 10 to 12 inches in depth. Beyond the emotional aura, the mental aura may fluctuate somewhat. If it becomes narrower, it will become correspondingly denser.

In contrast with the variety of using the emotional aura, the mental auras are there to color the yellow of intellect and the orange of intuition or a single golden color, a blending of the two. When it comes to colors, the outer layer, which is closer to external stimuli, will respond fastest. When the yellow is on the outside, then the person operates intellectually and does not allow the golden orange of intuition to come out when orange is on the outside. It means that the intuitive function is stronger than the intellectual. Because we referred to this aura as the mental aura, you might assume that this band would reflect the activity of the total mind, but it does not. The mental aura reflects only the activity of the conscious and the subconscious mind, the conscious being the intellect and the subconscious being the coordinator of physiological activity, the maker of dreams, the archives and library.

When the mental aura is a single color, a golden yellow blending of the conscious and the subconscious, it means that the person is operating with synchronized, conscious and subconscious minds. That is, the subconscious works with unconscious intuition and brings it to the surface and registers it there. When the two colors are blended into a single color, physiological changes will take place because volunteer control is possible. Such a person would be producing predominantly alpha brain waves because alpha is the brainwave of self regulation. The poorer countries the next hour reflect the activity of what some people have called the super conscious mind or what I call the conscious mind.

This is the individual as part of the universal mind, the pure creative intuition, the very conscious mind, besides representing your higher consciousness, also represents the universal collective of consciousness. The conscious mind is associated with the slow brain waves of Theta and Delta. When these brain waves are present, there's hypnagogic imagery that cannot be altered by conscious spoliation. The long wavelengths of conscious activity put you constantly in communication with the outer environment, including the physical environment. These wavelengths are so long that they go far beyond the physical plane of the Earth. It is for this reason that your conscious aura is your individual picture of what is happening in the universe, whether or not you're aware of it.

The very conscious aura contains the same seven main colors of the chakras, the colors are not necessarily where the chakras are except for wanting the gold of the heart chakra. Even though the same colors may occur in the conscious aura and the emotional aura, there's a difference between them.

Chapter - 22

The poorer countries are wider in size than the emotional, approximately 12 to 18 inches. And the colors are always lighter, more pastel. Their colors are very rarely seen in the conscious aura because it is a part of the mind that is universal, the higher consciousness, and that has not been touched yet by the individual shortcomings, by the activities of day to day X. In the very conscious brain, you're always growing and progressing, although you may never become aware of it or learn to express your growth. The Rangers are therefore never stagnant because of the continuous action going on in this area.

The colors are never dense or dark. If you will recall the image of Pascale's communicating vessels, which I discussed, and voluntary controls, you will remember that when three vessels are all open and connected to each other, food that is poured into one vessel will flow into and full all through to an equal level. When pressure is put on the surface of the liquid, one of the vessels, the flow into the adjacent vessel will be blocked in the same way mental blockages will prevent our intuitive knowledge from flowing out of the conscious mind into the subconscious and the conscious minds. All our traumas are actually like a surface pressure, a suppression of the flow of information from the universal mind. So even though you keep on moving and developing on a universal plane, you might not see any indication of it, even though you are in constant communication with the universe at large throughout your conscious mind, you will not be aware of it unless you release the energies and avoid putting pressure on the subconscious mind.

This is why the cosmic view as a part of nightly meditation empties out those vessels that have pressure on them and restores intuitive flow. Compared with the emotional aura, the conscious are as much lighter, reflecting greater brilliance and intuitiveness for the martial arts to look like the pair conscious would mean to integrate the colors to become more transpersonal. The most favorable state would have to be the emotional area exactly equal to the conscious aura, which would mean that the person is emotionally expressing what the soul actually dictates. In such a case, the mental aura would be one integrated color and we would see a merging of the three R's together. Is it possible for us personally to do anything to increase the action of the conscious mind on the rest? If we go into theta brain waves, we become aware of what is going on in the conscious. There are a number of techniques being explored for voluntarily going into theta, both with the mechanical assistance of biofeedback instruments and in meditation centers without the use of instruments.

When people learn to go into the theater, brain waves at will, they become more intuitive, creative? The calls are. We know very little about the cause or because it is so subtle, we might also call this the soul ammunition because it deals with the soul essence, the individual's capacity of energy that we call the soul. This is the aura in which the very first becomes visible, because it is in this aura that all the experiences you've gone through as a soul or capacity of energy led to the absorption of various frequencies and aptitudes. Out of the pure white light, that is your input, what is left after it hits the prism of the causal aura is the way you operate on or what I have called your toolbox. If the calls show what your soul essence has experienced, the ratios, all the potentials of what you have not yet experienced. I very rarely see more than two and at most three colors in the casual area.

At first, I understood very little about the meaning of the colors in this aura, but through years of observation and of questioning of the people who are, as I observed, I've come to some understanding of it. It is the result of the source of your being, your whole being is depending on that substance, what we call so. The colors represent the different qualities of energy, of experience and what we might call formal life experiences. When I say former life experience, I do not necessarily mean life in a human body on this planet. I'm talking about life experience of energy in what form it may have been. I do not know. I personally believe and I know from experience with a two year regression research project that there is such a thing as reincarnation and that it might be possible to go into another physical body after leaving this one. But if we look at it from the context of universal time, it would seem rather silly for us on this one small planet Earth to remain in just one place, in just one form of physical body where we're surrounded by a huge galaxy, one of billions of galaxies.

Well, we see some white color in the causal air aura. To me, it means no physical existence in any form, a sort of suspended animation, pure energy activity without specific material form. This would represent a period when your beingness was pure light, in essence, before it became individualized. Before there was any consciousness of its own individuality. The actual colors we observe in the causal aura may represent the last stages of the person's physical appearance, the memory patterns of the very characteristic of the person in previous life. Examples. If a person has been in the area, for example, we might assume that that person had a life of service because pink is the color of love, of service, of nursing and nursing humankind's. If there was more of a reddish glow, the person would have been some sort of an artist with inspirational energy of the red color of life force. If the color was pure yellow, I would say the person had been very scientific and probably also very tedious.

I have observed an interesting way that colors appear in the causal aura, which I call the isle or Island. If we look at one of these islands in three dimensions, it will appear to be a dense colored band around the person at a certain level of the body, but with a different color completely surrounding that band. In cross chapter or in two dimensional representation, this island will look like a cable with the center one color and the insulation, another color. Over the years, I've come to get a feeling for the meaning of these islands, they seem to represent events in the past in which the soul was held back from expressing something. A person once came to me for counseling and I saw this causality or a purple area with red around it. I said to the person, you cannot deal with any organized religion, can you? Oh, no, he replied, I've tried everything, but I cannot handle any organized religion also,

I went on, you cannot really deal with anything else that is organized.

You're always rebelling against anything that imposes authority beyond your own authority. And the person had to admit what I said was true. I explained my observations on the basis of what I had seen in the causal aura. It seems that there was a stage of your life where you were forced by vital force, by physical force to integrate whatever and whatever that might have been. The edge around the purple meant that there was force applied. On another occasion, I was counseling a man to whom I said, you must have problems with money, you can't hold onto money. He said, yeah, you're right, one hand gets money and it's already spent by the other. It never warms my right hand because it's already been handed out by my left. I hate money, I don't want to have anything to do with it, but how do you know? I said, you have a brown island in your calls with red around it, metaphorically, I might say you must have been a tax collector in your former life. In this life, you don't want anything to do with money because you were forced to deal with it in the past.

If we saw Yellow Island with a green band around it, the green band would represent growth, evolution, preservation for the sake of preservation. That person was totally involved in the rationale. That is how I use the calls in counseling. There is very little more I can tell you about it. However, we must be careful when we talk about former existences because past lives are certainly not the only explanation for some of the knowledge that people have of events from the past. What investigation concerning a four year old Turkish boy who claimed that he had been murdered? He went several hundred miles away from where he was living and pointed out a barn where he claimed the body was buried. Investigators found the body there.

The boy pointed out the person he claimed murdered him. In his former life, he had been the father of four adult sons, and as soon as he returned to the family's farm, he began to rule and regulate the entire household, including his former wife. As a boy, four or five years old, he ruled the household like an adult of fifty two who had been murdered. In our investigations of past life experiences, we're very rarely seen a person who has come back with a span of less than seven hundred or eight hundred years. Therefore, I suggest we be very cautious about life readers who report 10 lives for a subject in two or three centuries, the only instances in which people seem to come back sooner than seven hundred or eight hundred years is when they have been victims of violent death, accidental death, murder or suicide. For two years, I was myself involved as a subject under regression every Sunday morning, from nine o'clock to one o'clock, I was under hypnosis.

We cannot find any life experiences between this present one and one that was in five hundred and fifty B.C., I was a gypsy observer and I spoke Arabic during the hypnotic chapters. The researchers could not understand me. They did not even know what language I was speaking. Finally, they borrowed some Arabic dictionaries and started reading words out to me. I did not understand what they were saying, but I was correcting their pronunciation. At last, they brought in medals and you see a psychologist who lives in Ojai, California, to speak Arabic to me and I answer them. Three weeks before he was brought in, I had stated that I was a barber, that it was five hundred and fifty B.C. and that I lived in a certain area in the mountains. When you came to talk to me, you said you could not understand what I was saying because I was speaking in a Berber dialect that had not been spoken since three hundred B.C., that was quite a confirmation. However, this does not necessarily prove a former life. It may be possible to resonate with occurrences out of the past to be in tune physically with someone else's life as if it were your own. So we must be very careful not to jump to conclusions about past lives on the basis of such evidence.

The cosmic spiritual areas. The cosmic and spiritual auras. The actual names are interchangeable, and are very difficult to see. I can say very little about them because I have not yet learned very much about what they mean, although I'm sure eventually we may be able to observe more about them. However, I have observed cases in which these auras have a definite meaning. Over the last several years, I've seen more and more people who have a very bright cosmic field. These people have been younger people, the so-called flower children of the coming age of Aquarius. When I have been able to distinguish the base colors of the cosmic field in these young people, something distinctive has made them stand out. What I've seen in that base color that sets them apart is a very fine gold sparkle like gold dust, giving the field a slight iridescence. The base color might be a very subtle fine green or very subtle purple or blue, but they all have the same gold and sparkles. It is as if you were in a dark room and the sun was shining through a slit in the curtain.

A ray of light comes through streaming into the dark room and you see all the dust particles floating in it and in their motion, these dust particles twinkle like little golden speckles. That is what I have seen in these people's cosmetic or spiritual areas. I began to notice that there was something in common among all these people, these golden specks of cosmic fields are found only in the younger generation and all the people who love them seem to have similar feelings. In counseling chapters, they express the feeling that they do not belong on this planet Earth, that they do not know what they're supposed to be doing here. They seem to be wondering what they are doing here as if they are all strangers in a strange land. I suggest that these people are sold, incarnated from perhaps some other planet or of a high spiritual quality who have difficulty adapting to the values of this planet.

My eldest child, who is now nine years old, is one of these Aquarian children with a gold speckled or. She's very headstrong and already seems to be setting herself up as my teacher.

Chapter - 23

And always knowing this, that seems beyond even the uncanny wisdom characteristics of children. When my wife was pregnant, I could see this gold speckled aura emanating from her belly and I knew the child would be one of these cosmic souls. Auric diagnosis. Before I proceed with the discussion of how the aura can be used in diagnosing illness, let me emphasize something that I already have said and that I will repeat throughout this book. It is very important to understand that before you can see anyone else's energy field, you will have to look through your own. So your own had better be very, very subtle or transparent.

For example, let us assume that someone wakes me up at six thirty a.mIn just a half hour, I went to sleep. I need very little sleep and often do not go to bed until nearly done. Asking me to tell him what is in his energy field, I might say to him, my, you certainly have a dark energy field around you. What I'm actually seeing, Of course, is the results of my own energy field, which is dark and murky. I have not even pulled out the curtains yet and the fog has not lifted from my consciousness. If you're going to use the OR as a diagnostic tool, we must always have our own energy field under perfect observation and we must never make a statement about anyone else's aura unless our own is so bright and transparent that it is clear glass. If you're sick or tired, that is not the time to observe anyone else's energy field. It has always amazed me to see people whose bodies are sick and deformed from the careless way they live, from improper diet and lack of discipline, who see other people, this is wrong with you and that's wrong with you.

I know they have to look through their own energy fields first. And quite often I wonder if they're not telling the other person some of the things they're seeing in their own hours. So I caution you to be very careful, to be very sure that you are aware of your own energy field before you try to interpret what you see in that of another person. Thus far, we have discussed each of the lower layers of the aura as a separate indication of what is going on in an individual's physical, emotional, mental or spiritual state. In reality, Of course, all the layers of the aura are interrelated. What I say there is a brownish, murky bronze color around the heart, emotional. There are still some gold Nooran showing through, but the color is largely dark and muddy. This means that there is some disease in the heart area. Of course, this heart disease will show up on the physical level as well.

The physical aura, as you know, has no colors in it. But around the region of the heart and the thymus gland, you will observe dark spots in the physical area when we see a dark multicolor in the heart region and the emotional aura. We know we have to look at the physical heart and thymus gland as well. On the other hand, you might discover the disorder first and the physical aura, and you will then know that the emotional aura is also dark in the same area. There is a correlation in every physiological condition. It is impossible to have a beautiful, glowing, subtle, emotional aura when you have a terribly sick body. We therefore have several cross references when we observe the aura. The only part of the art that has no cross references is a pair of consciousnesses taken by itself because of their conscious aura, representing the person's condition in his or her unconscious state. If, however, the mental orishas, a single blended color with some merging with the pair of conscious aaargh, then we know that the person has brought some of the aspects of his or her unconscious rudimental into the emotional and that the emotional similarly will affect the physiological state.

The reverse is, Of course, also possible, the physiological state of a person may get better and the emotional aura will get clearer, which will make it easier to work with a blended mind and there will be a blending of the colors and the mental aura. I've seen some individuals whose emotional hours are mirror images of their conscious auras, such an aura marks a very high type of person. There are many saints walking among us in all stages of life, from garbagemen to physicians to holy men. But the saints of healthy bodies. We have all heard stories about people who have become spiritual leaders and who have allowed their bodies to take on the karma of other people and who have died of some disease such as cancer. This makes no sense. I cannot take your karma upon my own shoulders. You cannot escape your karma no matter what, because only you can do your own chapters. If I do your homework for you, you will not have learned anything from it, the only way you can graduate is by doing your own homework to graduate from your own ignorance.

Therefore, people who proclaim that they take on others for the love of them do not really love their fellow humans deeply enough. Let us take a detailed look at a hypothetical case in which the hour is used in diagnosis, a variety of colors can be seen in the emotional aura. Remember that these colors actually form three dimensional bands around the physical body. They're not two dimensional, as in the drawing. What can we tell about this person on the basis of their colors and the emotional aura? In the area of the root chakra is the color blue, which is the color of the throat chakra and represents expressive energy, or will power in this case, will power is being used not to express energy, but to hold it back to repress it. When the movement is down, going below the throat chakra, you know, will power is being pushed down and suppression is taking place.

In this person, the world power is being used to suppress the sexual energy of the root chakra. Around the solar plexus area, we see the color pink. Think is the color of love or reserve energy. A lot of extra emotional energy is being pumped into the solar plexus area. And so the person is in a highly emotional state. But these emotions have not penetrated further up an underground transmutation at the heart chakra where they would be turned into solar energies. Such heightened emotionality in the solar plexus area, as you know, can lead to physical problems such as indigestion and ulcers. Purple, the color of integration or spirituality, is that the area of the throat chakra, it is that this chakra that energies are expressed through volition. This is the sort of person who will act as if everything has to be spiritual, but who misunderstands the meaning of spirituality.

He or she is bringing the purple from the crown chakra down to the throat chakra where he or she is trying to bring it out, so this person is trying to express the spiritual, but he or she is not really living it. This person also has pure yellow above his or her head for the sake of simplicity. We have eliminated the rate in this drawing. So the yellow is in the emotion area rather than presenting the right. I found that when a person is in danger, a lot of the time there is a kind of yellowish glow around the brain when he or she is an alpha. There is a bluish glow around the brain in theta there is a purplish glow and in Delta the ammunition becomes a whitish gray or silver gray. Even the Menninger Foundation has confirmed that D.C. blows around the brain when a person is an alpha, although they have not been able to confirm the other colors for me.

The person in the drawing has pure yellow above his or her head, so he or she is in a great deal of the time. His or her crown chakra is radiating purple, but only at the area where he or she is trying to express it. The yellow, which is associated with consciousness, with the heart chakra he or she is trying to bring up toward the pineal gland so he or she has his or her heart on top of his or her pineal gland on top of his or her head. Is consciousness all located at the top of the head, which indicates a lot of cerebral action? Between the yellow at the top of the head and the purple in the throat area, we see green in the area of the pituitary or the brow chakra. Green is the color of the solar plexus and carries the idea. I want to grow. But how is this person growing here or she is not giving up his or her life preserving energy, but is keeping them all to him or herself? He or she is like a rose in a garden surrounded by thousands of other roses.

Who says I want to grow? I want all the food. This person is a narcissist. He or she holds everything in and wants to grow only spiritually. Somehow he or she has got the idea that his or her body does not need to be involved in this growth. He or she has emotions from the solar plexus growth state all bound up with his or her concern about spiritual growth. He or she is probably one of those starry eyed people who does not feel he or she needs to be involved from below to release his or her energies, he or she is very unrealistic. A person with such color in the emotional aura would be expected to be physically in a tight, rigid state, his or her problems will show up not only in the emotional aura, but also in the physical aura.

As you can see in the chart on the cover, there are dark spots around all the joints in the physical aura. This person has arthritis, a stiffness and rigidity in the joints here. She also has stomach problems. His or her energy is so clouded up that he or she has a dark band around the waist and the solar plexus area in the physical aura. He or she will probably have problems with constipation as well and will undoubtedly have sexual problems. If the person is male, he may have prostate troubles, for example. All of his or her sexual energy is being kept out and cannot move up in a healthy expression of energy flow. Furthermore, because of the emotional and mental state this individual is in, he or she is constantly in the beta brainwaves and is susceptible to migraines. The energies are all in the cerebral area, as we noted in Chapter one, such excessive cerebral activity also draws the blood to the brain, resulting in bad circulation to the rest of the body.

Well, we might see in the mental aura of our hypothetical patient. This person operates intellectually and does not allow his or her intuition to come out at all, he or she holds it in. In such a case, the inner part of the mental aura will be deep, dark orange and the outer part will be very bright yellow. If the person improves after treatment, the colors will blend and the mental aura would be a beautiful golden yellow if the colors are reversed. This will be a totally intuitive person who is not able to use the rational mind to put his or her intuitions into expression to make them a reality. Was that one glass or vision that committed us to observe an individual's mental, emotional and physical states? Of course, you would not want to restrict yourself to observing the physical, emotional and mental art. You would go on to the cell as well. What would the therapist do when confronted by the subject on the cover? The only way to communicate with such a person is by some other than verbal means, you cannot talk with such persons. They have their own opinions and are not interested in hearing yours.

So the first thing you would do in a therapy chapter is bombard him or her with bright white light that not only protects him or her from you, but also protects you from him or her. When I stand in front of a class, I do not want the students' problems to disturb me. I bombard the class with bright white light, which means that I first have to activate it and get it moving and get it out so that it is very beneficial for me. At the same time, I become attached and whatever is happening happens in the white light and I cannot be affected by it in a negative way. I expand myself throughout the room with all that energy so that the class will feel me so that my being this will affect everyone in the room. Anyone who deals with health must radiate his or her health out of him or herself. So if a person comes to you for help, you must first bombard that person with light and bombard the room you're working in with light. It is as if you have to be in a state of excitation all the time.

When I'm traveling and arrive in a new hotel room, I do not want to be involved in what went on there before me, so I won't watch the room by shining white light into it. Wherever I go, I'm constantly whitewashing. And if that does not work fast enough, I will also chant the. Sam has the same effect, it breaks down all the densities of energy around you. You can tell on therapy when you are having an effect on a person, you have embraced the person with the white light which starts to regenerate his or her systems, not verbalization, is needed to accomplish this. If the person does not get lighter in color, then your energy is not working. It is not high enough to regenerate that person. Maybe you do not have enough energy available at that moment to help regenerate that person.

Dating events from the Aaargh! Through many years of observation, I've discovered another interesting source of information in the human energy field, what I call the growth pattern in the aura. From below the central area, down into the ground where you cannot see the aura anymore, the emotional aura is a brownish green color, usually somewhat lighter toward the outside. It is in this part of the emotional aura that we can observe the growth pattern. We can see vortices which are also slightly visible in the physical aura, including the ovum through experience. I've learned that these sources of energy surrounding a person are like growth rings in trees and that each ring represents a year in time. Let us say that suddenly, four years ago, our subject had a spiritual rebirth, a tremendous transition in his or her life. In the growth area, the aura would begin from that point on to look at lighter green. It might be Kelly Green to start and where the rebirth occurred, it would suddenly get smaller, more of a charterer's color and you can start to count lines in it because every line becomes a solid color.

It is therefore possible to determine the approximate date at which important events took place or when a disease started by counting back on these growth rings. If the change took place four and a half years ago, the color change will be seen four and a half lines in from the outer part of the emotional aura. The flow of energies and auricular color theory. In Chapter one, we saw that light is a form of nourishment for the human organism and that as it moves down through the chakras, it is broken down into different qualities that nourish the different systems of the body. Below the heart, the light becomes progressively denser and more material, it then goes through a process of activation in the generative system at the root chakra. Practically all diseases have their foundation in this basement area where energies have taken on their densest form and not enough filtering may take place in density. I often call this area where energy exchange tends to get bogged down by the molasses. Other moves, as it moves up, it becomes more fluid and past the heart chakra, it becomes light.

The process then is from light to fire to substance or from substance to fire to light. If you bring life down, for example, if you bring the purple from the crown chakra down to the solar plexus, it will look darker and more dense in the emotional aura. Dark money colors show the influence of higher colors that actually cannot function lower down. So we really need to bring the lower ones up to make them lighter, not the higher ones down to make them denser. The normal process is a flow in and through and out and anything that tries to make a bypass from the Crown Center to the solar plexus, for example, forgetting about the throat in the heart, will produce a stagnation and will impede the healthy flow of energies. The energies have to go through the heart, and after they have gone down through the heart, they become denser. We've seen an emotional aura that when the colors of the higher chakras have been brought down, that means you're repressing the energies.

Take an example of the opposite case. What would it mean if a person brings a pink up around the shoulders? Pink is the color of emotion when we see a lot of pink in the emotional aura. We know we're dealing with a highly emotional individual, but now the pink is up around the shoulders at the level of the throat chakra. The throat chakra is no longer blue. It is now pink. Such a person no longer has sympathy for empathy, he or she has brought his or her emotions up through the heart chakra, the scene of consciousness, and is now expressing them. This is a desirable state of affairs. The ideal situation is to have the Choco's work upward in their expression and the emotional aura. It is a good sign, for example, for food to be seen above the throat chakra. Now the willpower is directed to a higher order of things. In philosophical terms, we might label the state as being not my will anymore, but they will. That will be done.

This is moving toward the transpersonal state, on the other hand, whenever the blue goes below the throat chakra, you know, will power is being pushed down and suppression or repression is taking place. Let us suppose that we see a very bright orange in the heart chakra, this indicates that the red orange has moved from the gonad area through the pink of the spleen chakra and the green of the solar plexus and is now bombarding the heart chakra. Such a person is inflamed. He or she has become transpersonal, meaning that he or she has gone beyond his or her own personality. He or she is this identifying with his or her own personality and is now identifying with his or her universal self. In other words, with his or her divine self. Higher self or God self. However, this is not the high state when a person reaches consciousness, which simply means a state of enlightenment, there is no fire anymore. There's only light. We see the pure white of saintliness, the halo.

How much higher states of consciousness appear in the conscious aura, let us say that we see pink in the solar plexus area in the conscious aura, pink is the color of emotion, of love, energy when the pink has moved up to the solar plexus area. That means that the solar plexus is now under the influence of this energy. The aura only reflects what is actually happening in you, although in this case it may be largely unconscious. When the pink is in the solar plexus area, you feel what has been described as a vexation of spirit, a longing, a craving to be with a higher power. The difference between a normal physically based emotional state and a pair of conscious emotional states is that the unconscious state involves lower frequencies and higher amplitude of energy. This is why we say we are in touch with the unattainable what we're having a peak experience. In such a state, we might see a very bright gold in the heart area of the conscious aura and the beautiful pink in the solar plexus area, the emotional energy represented by the color pink is being used not to express physically based drives, but rather to get in touch with a higher power with what we might call God or Spirit.

This is still an emotional experience, so grounded in the physical body, but it is a condition of joy, a high peak experience preparing to see the aura. In Chapter four, I will describe some exercises that will improve your physical vision and therefore help you to see the human aura. You may still have some questions about how the order really looks, you might think that because the various arms are in layers one over the other, you would not be able to distinguish which layers which. Actually, it is like looking through a very transparent jawbreaker. Candy made up of different colors and flavors, even though you have an outer layer of color on the outside, is so subtle that when you look further into the next one, the density is different and therefore you can distinguish one layer from another. The various layers of density will be particularly visible if you look at a person from the side. It does become more difficult to distinguish the layers when they start to merge, when one layer becomes so highly charged that the next starts to blend with it.

For example, when the emotional aura begins to burn with the mantle, and then you also start to see a merging of the mantle with the pair of consciousness. When you see this, you know, the person is fulfilling his or her purpose, that what comes through intuitively is directing his or her mind and actions and that his or her emotions are regulated by his or her unconscious, power conscious mind. This is a good thing to see what you would see in the physical aura in such a case is the area becoming brighter and brighter, the ground becoming wider and the ovum becoming much lighter and subtler until it becomes a cleaner, paler Ivry than it was before. Even in such a case, you can look through the aura and distinguish the different layers once you learn to see them. When you use meditation exercises to raise your energy patterns so that your consciousness and your energy are expanding, you're automatically going to affect all the different layers of your aura. It all becomes brighter until eventually the layers start blending.

The ideal situation would be if there were only one layer no longer divided into different densities or subtleties. Of course, the closer you can come to having such a high level of energy, such a blending of your own aura, the more accurate your perceptions of the energy fields around other people will be. This is why it is important to be healthy, not only physically healthy, but mentally, emotionally and spiritually healthy when we attempt to observe the hours of others.

Chapter - 24

For eye exercises for Orrock Vision. The physiology of expanded vision. Human beings generally use only a small percentage of the light that enters the eye because of improper use of the eyes, laziness and ignorance of the function, it has been said that only 10 percent of the light that enters the eye is actually utilized. When light enters the eye, it hits the retina in which two different types of cells are found, the rods deal with light and dark perception. They are highly sensitive to the presence of light but cannot respond to color.

The cones are concerned with color vision. There are three different types of cones which respond respectfully to yellow, blue and red wavelengths. When my strikes, the retina in its energy is absorbed by the rods and cones in the area it hits. There is a pigment in the rods and presumably in the cones. Also that when light is absorbed by the rod breaks down into simpler compounds. The pigment bleaches out during this breakdown, changing from purple to a yellowish color. Something in this chain of events triggers a release of electrical energy. The energy released in this manner by the rods and cones moves through the optic nerve. The optic nerve is different from any other nerve in the body. It is like a tunnel actually made up of many individual nerve fibers. The energy carried by the optic nerve activates the brain and according to the frequencies and amplitudes of the light that has entered the eye, starts a certain.

The rain radiates out this rhythmic energy, which is now synthesized on the visual area of the cerebral cortex, which is your screen. As soon as these synthesized pictures reflected back, you say, I see. How can we increase the activity of the rods and cones by activating the muscles of the eyelids and of the eye itself? We expose a greater number of rods and cones to incoming light because the light will not be hitting just one focal point on the retina. The exercises described in this chapter are intended to teach you to use the muscles of your eyes, thereby stimulating more rods and cones. The more energy that gets from the eye is into the optic nerve, the more the brain will be activated. The screen can therefore synthesize more than it did before and you will see more. Physics tells us that the visible spectrum is from a wavelength of four hundred nanometres to a wavelength of seven hundred nanometres. However, these limits represent an average. Certainly there are people with no particular gifts who can see higher or lower than this range.

One of the things that limits our ability to see beyond the so-called visible spectrum is our mental acceptance that we cannot see beyond the range. So if we let go of that preconception about the limitations of our visual ability, we should be able to expand the range of our vision. Sometime ago, I was involved in an experiment with Professor John Adams, a geophysicist at the University of Washington in Seattle, who interprets the infrared pictures of the geological situation on Earth that have been taken from satellites. In his laboratory he participated in a visual experiment in which he sent out a ray of light, and I told them when I started seeing it and what I saw, he recorded my observations on a computerized graph that was synchronized with the record of frequencies of the light he sent out. And when we later looked at the graph, it showed that I had been able to see light from three hundred and thirty five nanometres, which is in the short wave or ultraviolet range.

Sixty five nanometers below the visible spectrum, up to one thousand seven hundred nanometres, which is in the infrared one thousand nanometers above the visible spectrum. Professor Adams also tried the experiment and was amazed to discover that although he could not see in the ultraviolet, he was able to get up to one thousand three hundred thirty five, well beyond the visible spectrum. To do this, he had to throw away a previous concept and keep an open mind. Then he, too, was able to experience this expanded vision. The I exercise is described in this chapter, can expand your vision if you're able to keep an open mind about the possibilities. These are purely physiological, not metaphysical exercises. There is a certain amount of discipline involved in learning to do the exercises correctly without trying too hard to see some results.

The breathing exercises that should proceed. The exercises will similarly help to activate your system by providing plenty of oxygen. Taken all together, these exercises should result in brighter color vision and increased perception, even if you never see auras after doing these exercises, you should at least gain an improvement in your eyesight provided that you work at it. General instructions for the exercises in dealing with human error. There are two notions we must overcome. First, you have probably been told that such things do not exist, so you will have to deal with your own limiting belief system. Second, you may have been told that even if the aura does exist, you will never be able to see it. The purpose of working with the eye charts described in this chapter is to improve your vision, to increase the muscular control and strength of the eyes and thereby stimulate the rods and cones to a greater degree.

By strengthening your vision, the eye exercises can help you to see auras. Research may eventually confirm my own suspicion based on my observations over more than thirty five years that whereas most people use only 15 or 20 percent of the available rods and cones in their eyes, people with Arc Vision use perhaps thirty five percent or more of the available loans and cones. The charts are simply a guide to help you learn to control your eyes if you discover you can control your eyes and the way suggested without the charts, so much the better the charts are for those people who need some help to discover the abilities. These exercises must be faced with a warning, do not imagine that you can use these methods lightly. This work requires your sincere cooperation.

If the purpose of doing these exercises is to make you capable of observing human energies, you must be sincere in your desire first for self-improvement and second for getting to know your fellow humans better and to interact with them and help them. Observing human energies can be an especially valuable diagnostic and therapeutic tool for people who are involved in the health professions and in counseling. These exercises should be done every day, otherwise you will have no way of knowing if you're really improving, the chance should be used at home whenever you're free of all distractions. Do the exercises in a very well lit room because you need reflection but avoid any glare with all these exercises. The harder you try, the less you'll experience. Results come from intense concentration with that coalition, a state of consciousness generally corresponding to the low alpha and theta frequencies.

Using the dimensions given, make your own charts out of construction paper, the charts should be hung on a wall that is free from distraction objects with the center of each chart at eye level and about six feet away from you. There are four charts, each has a different role that excites your perception of color. I have also included a breathing exercise, the lion's breath that should proceed each exercise, as well as two finger exercises to supplement the benefits to your eye muscles. Charge one, two and four are all black and white. You might think that in order to see color, the charts should have color in them. But Black has absorbed all the colors and light and white reflects all the lights on, black and white, all the colors are there. It is up to you to discover them and take them out of their black or white state. If you wear glasses, you should do the zooming exercises and the other exercises with your glasses on, if you wear contact lenses, you should remove them during the eye exercises as well as during the lion's breath.

When you become capable of doing the exercises regularly and have some feeling that you are perceiving more clearly, remove your glasses and see if you can achieve the same results without them, perhaps with a little extra effort. These exercises can improve your vision in general, as well as enable you to see auras. Once you become familiar with the kinds of muscular and visual activities that are stimulated by the charts, you can use a tree or a point on the wall or something on the horizon and do the same things with them that you do with the charts. However, the charts give you a point of concentration and discipline by teaching you to stay within the limits of the design on the chart. When you work with these charts every day, you will begin to see faint fuzzy colors, which you may immediately discount as being the result of muscle strain, or afterimages yet the colors you're looking for will at first come in precisely this manner.

One way to distinguish afterimages is that they will always float in front of the chart. If you see colors in the same plane as the chart, passive attention, after some progress, you may go through a stage where you will see rainbows everywhere. Because of the intense gazing involved in these exercises, you may see images or colors from the charts superimposed on the wall or an empty space when you suddenly look away from the chart. This stage will pass. These are after images of what you saw on the charts and maybe your first indication that you're beginning to get some results. As you go through the exercises, make smaller copies of the charts on white paper, as you begin to see colors, use crayons or colored pencils to duplicate on these charts what you have observed in doing the exercises. This is very important because if and when your new visual experiences start occurring, you may doubt whether you're observing something different from what you used to see.

By marking down your color experiences and copies of the charts as they occurred to you, you will have a record of your progress. This feedback will help you to gain confidence in your organism and its powers. In the instructions that follow, I first give the exercises to be done with each of the charts, but I do not say what you're likely to observe in this way. I avoid giving you any suggestions in a separate chapter feedback from our charts, you will find descriptions of the color experiences you are likely to have. Work with the charts to observe colors in them for yourself before you read the descriptions in the feedback chapter. Under no circumstances should you do these exercises longer than 10 or 15 minutes at a time. Take a rest for about 20 minutes at the end of an exercise period of fatigue, we'll tell you when to stop because you're exercising the muscles of your eyes more vigorously than you're accustomed to doing. Ideally, the exercises should not need to be done more than twice a day in the morning and at night, for example, the charge should be used in the order given with sufficient rest after each.

I would not recommend that you go on to the later exercises until you have seen at least some colors with chart one. However, if you have repeatedly tried chart one and then chart two for 10 or 15 minutes each with very little results, then go on to chart three, which is the easiest to get results with. Then when you go back to the earlier charts, you may see something there and that will encourage you breathing exercise. Lion's breath. Before doing the exercises with the chart, it is always recommended that you do the breathing exercises taught in voluntary controls, namely paradoxical breathing, or if you're not able to sustain paradoxical breathing, diaphragmatic breathing, it is very important to do these breathing exercises because the activation of your system, including your eyes, depends on the proper fuel oxygen.

After doing the general breathing exercises, you should next do a special breathing exercise derived from yoga known as the Lion's Breath. This exercise is specifically designed to force oxygen into the head and behind the eyes. When you first try the line breath, you might want to check for an improvement in your vision by looking at a colored object in your surroundings before you begin and then looking at it after doing the breathing exercise. Immediately after doing the lion's breath, you will find that the eyes have become relaxed and everything looks brighter. As with the exercises themselves, even if this breathing exercise does not lead ultimately to your being able to see auras, it can at least produce an improvement in your eyesight if you practice it regularly. The lion's breath should be done in the sitting position because it may affect your equilibrium, so we take a deep breath using your abdomen to suck in the air. And then bring the air up as if to exhale. But instead, put a throat lock on the breath and gag. In the beginning, you will probably make some sound effects as you gag, so you may want to do this in privacy.

As you become accustomed to the exercise, you will learn that it is not necessary to make a gagging noise. In the classical yoga posture, the tongue is thrust backward to heighten the gag effect. For this exercise, you do not need to go that far. Instead of thrusting the tongue backwards, you stick it out. The more you gag, the more your tongue will stick out again. Hold your breath. Act as if you're going to exhale, but hold it back and force it up into the skull cavities instead.

You can practice this exercise at other times during the day, for example, whatever you go to the bathroom, it will help your bowel movements and improve your circulation. So go ahead and gag a little. If you wear glasses, you can keep them on during this exercise as long as they do not pop off your nose. If you wear contact lenses, take them out, although you may need to replace them for the later eye exercises, at least at first, until you can do without them. Description you can make out of construction paper.

Chapter - 25

Start with a 15 inch black square in the middle of this, put a nine inch white square finally in the middle of the white square, put a three inch black square place to start with the center at eye level, about six feet away on an uncluttered wall in a well room. Breathing exercise starts by doing the lion's breath to send oxygen to the brain and eyes. Step one, concentration and disintegration. Imagine a little white dot at the very center of the chart, focus your eyes on the imaginary center spot. When you're properly concentrated, you will be completely absorbed in the whole chart and be centered from everything around it.

At least at first, it will help if there are no distraction objects on the wall adjacent to the chart. Step two, zooming in. In order to learn to zoom in and zoom out on the chart, mentally, bring the chart towards you as if it were in motion coming toward you and past you. When this is done properly, the check will seem to become three dimensional, the squares will become cubes, and it will appear that you're looking through the interior of a billows that is moving past you as it expands. Then push it away from you mentally so that the bills appear to close and move away, the zoom effect is accomplished by using the muscles inside your eyes. When you're zooming in and zooming out on the chart, you will feel the effects on the muscles in your eyes. Step three, vertical sweep.

After you've established good zoomin contact with the chart, focus on the center of the chart with both eyes. Raise both your eyes with a broad sweep to the front of the chart. Imagine that the chart is the wall of the room and that you're looking up to the angle it makes with the ceiling. You must see all the charts and nothing but the charts without focusing on any one part and covering the whole area and the broad sweep. Next step down to the bottom edge, sweep your eyes up and down the chart. Imagine that your eyes are brooms and that you're sweeping the chart with equal force with each. I stay within the boundary of the black outer square. In the beginning, you will need to practice the sweeping motion very slowly. If one is stronger than the other, you might want to practice with the weaker eye alone to strengthen it. First, zoom in and zoom out, then close one eye and scan in a broad sweep with one eye, then the other working at each of them until both achieve the same speed once you've gotten the good speed going with each. I do the exercise with both eyes. Step four, horizontal sweep.

Do exactly the same sweeping motion, but now let both eyes sweep horizontally once again, making sure to take in all the charts. Go from the left edge to the right edge and back, you will notice that there is a difference in this pattern. When you move your eyes to the side, the outside, I will reach the edge first and the other eye will stop in the middle. Try to accept the feeling of being divided in half. Do not let one I lead or dominate. This is not easy, but it is a preparation for the next step. Step five, combine sweep. Combine the vertical and horizontal motion by starting at the bottom of the chart, going up to the center then out to the left edge. Then across to the right edge. Then back to the center, up to the top and back to the bottom. Although it sounds complicated, the pattern is actually quite easy. You can bury this combined motion, for example, starting at the top in the beginning. This will go very slowly. You will have to become comfortable with the early parts of the exercise before you can get up a good speed on the combined sweep. The goal of this exercise is to learn to do it quickly, because the more speed you achieve, the more you will start observing things that are not at first apparent in the chart. Speed will stimulate and excite the eyes.

At first, you will need a couple of 10 or 15 minute chapters on each separate movement before you can do them quickly and thoroughly enough to put them together into the combined sweep. Be sure to rest adequately after these 10 or 15 minute practice periods. Do not be impatient with yourself. You have used your eyes in this fashion very little, if at all, in your life. Once again, you can do the combined sweep fast enough and with proper concentration, you will begin to see colors. Record what you can see on a copy of the chart. Discipline is important in this exercise, the more you look for color, the less you will see because you put your thinking process in the way of pure response to stimulation. Even if you think you have seen no colors, you may perceive after images of colors, after you stop looking at the chart. This is the test achievement in the exercises. The afterimages are a reflection to what you were stimulated to see. If you did not see anything, there would be no afterimage. Another test is to look away from the chart and then look right back. If the pros and cons of your eyes were truly stimulated intensely, you may be able to see the colors briefly.

The feedback chapter will show what color is present you may experience when you work with the chart, but do not refer to that chapter until you have had the chance to observe some results for yourself. Some people will not get any results from this exercise at first, they need some more immediate feedback to see what is happening in their heads and their eyes when they're zooming. If you feel you're not getting any results from one, two part one of the finger exercise. Take your name to describe. This job consists of a white five pointed star on a 15 inch black square. From one point of the stars to its opposite point, along a straight line is 11 inches. The distance between adjacent points is about six three quarters inches, hitting the chart six feet away with its center at eye level breathing exercise. Do the lion's breath. Step one, zooming. Zoom in and out on the chart a couple of times until you have some familiarity with it, keep the whole chart and focus all the time, step to gaze and float it for count.

Start at a concentrated and decent trade on the point. Imagine that the point is the center of a circle about two inches in diameter and gaze at it for eight counts. In the black space between A and B, imagine four equally spaced points counting one, two, three, four. Look at each imaginary point as you float from A to B. Then look at B for eight counts again, imagining it to encircle with it. Point B as its center. Repeat the process flowing from one point to point on four counts until you return to a bingo immediately to point C gaze for eight counts and repeat the whole process. But this time going around the start in a counterclockwise direction. Rest for 15 to 20 counts. Step three, gaze and float for two counts. Repeat step two completely, but this time use four counts on the points of the start in two counts in between, . Step for gays and float to one count. Repeat the same process, but used to count on the points of the star and one in between.

After each stage of gazing and floating restaurant, 15 to 20 counts, after doing all four steps rest at least half an hour. Once you begin observing things, when you do this exercise, record the results on a copy of the chart, the feedback chapter describes what you should experience, but again, you're not looking at the chapter until you have gotten some results for yourself. Description, this chart consists of a five inch diameter circle of royal blue or dark powder blue on a 15 inch white square. Hang it six feet away with the center at eye level. Breathing exercise, do the lion's breath. Step one, zooming gaze at the center of the circle. Zoom in and out once you've established good, zoom in contact with the chart. You may start seeing some things. Step two, clockwise circle. Move the eyes around the edge of the blue circle faster and faster, try to follow the outer edge of the blue circle against the white background. In the beginning, you might move your head slightly so that you become aware of the feeling of the motion. Then do just with your eyes.

This will be rather slow at first, rest your eyes for a couple of seconds and repeat this part of the exercise, we're first focusing and zooming in and out, then moving around the circle clockwise. Before you try the next motion, which is counterclockwise, you will want to develop good clockwise speed, a good speed is 10 times around the circle in one minute. Step three, counterclockwise circle. Repeat the circular motion following the edge of the blue circle in a counterclockwise direction, getting the feeling of moving your eyes rather than your head. You must feel that your eyes are doing the rolling, although in the beginning you may feel some strain in your eye, muscles keep working for increased speed, moving in both clockwise and counterclockwise directions with adequate rest periods in between. After working with this chart, close your eyes and look at the after images, sometimes the colors around the circle will also appear as after images first, but they will be in the opposing colors.

As with all the charts, do not do this exercise for more than 10 or 15 minutes at a time, then rest at least 20 minutes. Record your results on a copy of the chart where you may experience what is described in the feedback chapter. Description, this chart, like the first two, is black and white with no colors, it consists of a black rectangle on the left, 15 inches by nine inches wide, side by side with a white rectangle of the same dimensions on the right. Inside the black rectangle is a white oval and inside the white rectangle is a white oval outlined in black inside the oval on the white side, but not the one on the black side is a black horizontal lens or shaped form, having this chart six feet away with its center at eye level. Breathing exercise, do the lion's breath.

Step one, zoom and sweep one side and both sides. One I. Cover one eye, focus the other eye on the left half of the chart, make the white oval, zoom in and zoom out, sweep that eye up and down on the left half of the chart, then have it sweep both sides together, up and down, step to zoom and sweep one side and both sides. I repeat the same steps with the other eye alone.

Step three, sweep the whole chart, both eyes. With both eyes sweep the whole chart up and down, avoid having one eye stay on one side of the chart work to increase your speed as you sweep faster and faster up and down, you may get the feeling of being cross eyed after doing this exercise because it is not easy. I advise doing it first with each separately to see which eye is more perceptive and more capable of doing it. Then do it with both eyes when you feel they are both perceiving equally. If you do the exercise and do not get any results, keep gazing at the chart passively for a few minutes, you're likely to get feedback. Then you need to be patient. Remember, your eyes are getting very tired from doing something they're not accustomed to. Record your observations on a copy of the chart. The colors you should perceive are discussed in the feedback chapter. Finger exercise, first, do the lion's breath, part one for people who need early feedback from zooming exercises. Try this finger exercise, hold one index finger a couple of inches away from your eyes and gaze at it, then put your other index finger in front of the first. Now, without paying any attention to the first closer finger, start moving the other finger away from you very slowly following it with your eyes.

Move this finger until it is at arm's length, then bring it back very slowly until it meets the first finger. You may see some strange phenomena during this finger exercise, perhaps a transparent finger or two or three fingers do not pay attention to these. After doing this exercise, you should be able to close your eyes, imagine your finger to be in front of you and reproduce in your mind's eye the experience of zooming in and out with the finger. When you open your eyes and try zooming with the chart, you should not have such difficulty. Part two. This part of the exercise, besides activating your rods and cones by increasing your eye movements, will also improve your peripheral vision. Extend the index finger of your right hand with the thumb tucked inside the palm. Place your index finger against your nose, so the knuckle touches your nostril. Then do the same thing on the other side of your nose with the left hand gaze at the right index finger. This may make you feel slightly cross-eyed eyed now, very slowly. Move the other finger straight away from you and look at this finger which is moving away.

Still very slowly bring the finger back, but instead of stopping, let it go past your eyes and follow it without turning your head. Keep following the finger as you move it around and behind your head. It is as if you are looking through your head. Now, bring the finger very slowly back to your nose. After you've done this a couple of times, switch hands and do the exercise with the opposite finger. The reason you focus on the first finger is to get your eyes to converge when you start to look at the finger that moves, you will lose sight of the stationary finger. Also, when you start to focus on the finger that moves away, it may extend itself visually so that two fingers are coming at you like a transparent image. You may see an energy field around your finger, which is its physical aura. As you continue to gaze at the finger, you may see a streak of light moving with it as though you're seeing an emerging field moving along with it. After a period of intense focusing, the moving finger may become a phantom finger entirely, only the fingernail and the tip of the finger being visible or your whole finger may disappear when you bring it back.

Of course, these results depend on the condition of your eyesight, along with the results described, everything will look brighter after you do the exercise. Feedback from the eye charts chart one, the colors and spectra you see in the horizontal sweep should be the same in the vertical sweep, but arranged differently. Of course, in the vertical sweep, the colors will appear as vertical rainbow in the white area to each side of the black center square. In the horizontal sweep, the rainbow will be horizontal in the way above and below the center black square. In the combined sweep, you will see interlacing rainbows, a checkerboard of colors throughout the entire white chapter, and eventually you will see a circle of colors like a color wheel. Try on the eight for count, you will probably not see anything but great on the four to count the imaginary circles around each point, take on a goldish white. When you move from point to point, you see a reddish pink glow in between. On the two counts, you begin to get the feeling that the star has changed into a circle. Later you see all the colors of the spectrum in the circle in the center of the white star. The lighter colors, light green, light pink, light blue, yellow will appear. On the outer part of the star, the darker colors, deep purple, blue, green appear.

As you speed up the count, you will see gray, gold and silver at the points, and as you further increase the tempo around the star, you may occasionally see golden flashes or sparks. In the white area, in the middle of the chart, some people see the image of an individual, a man or a woman or a baby. Such images are coming from the unconscious. The exercise has stimulated the unconscious mind through activation of the visual cortex, which begins to release some intuitive images that have nothing to do with this particular exercise. The mental image is simply being reflected on the visual cortex to counter such distractions, make an intensive effort at focusing first before you start to do the exercise itself in order to keep your eyes from playing optical games with you. Chart three, first, you will notice a golden sunburst all around the blue circle, second, the ball becomes three dimensional. You feel almost as if you can see behind it. Third, the faster you move your eyes, the more they seem to stand still as you go faster and faster. Eventually you will see colors arranged around the ball and equally spaced segments.

At the top is the red line going counterclockwise, the red turns into violet, then a white spot with changing colors, then blue, then green at the bottom, then yellow, then another white spot with changing colors. On the left, that orange. As you become even more proficient with this chart, the white background will look lavender purplish and the blue circle will look white. With faster motion around the circle, the spectrum will rotate according to the speed of the eye movement, as if there were three or four circles superimposed on each other, each of them having different colors that move in their places. However, the colors will remain in the same sequence in relation to each other as before. This is the easiest of the four eye charts because the results come faster than with the score of the start. With those two charts, you get many afterimages. There are afterimages with the circle too, but you can recognize them for what they are. Chart four on the left side, you will see a green eye in the same place and with the same shape as the black eye in the middle of the oval. In the next oval, you will see a concentrated, oval shaped ring of color next to the black background, beginning with the darker colors on the outside. Purple, indigo, blue, green.

As you get toward the center of the white oval, the colors are lighter yellow, orange, red. On the right side of the chart, the colors are reversed. The purple is on the inside and the red is on the outside. On the right side, you also see within the Oval a question shaped spectrum of color above and below the eye with the purple closest to the black of the eye and the red toward the outside. Observing the R.M.. What results can you expect from doing the exercises, the charts are, after all, inanimate objects, and so there is not much variety to be had in observing them later on, when you begin removing the energy fields around people, it will be an entirely different matter because there is such a great variety of changes taking place in human energy fields that it may be difficult to pick out even a general pattern in an individual.

One of my students working with the charts for about 20 minutes a day, found that at the end of five weeks of practice, he was able to see a few distinct colors around the subject. I was able to confirm those colors as part of the subject's aura. Training to see the aura is not a simple task.

Besides having the proper motivation and following the discipline of meditation, it is a matter of months or even years of working to improve your eyesight, not just a few weeks with the charts. Once you're properly prepared through exercise, meditation and a clear purpose, you will be ready to start observing human energy fields. What are the optimum conditions for seeking the aura? Some people claim that you can see the best in a dark room. The only thing you will see better under such conditions is the physical aura because that becomes translucent. But darkness absorbs the photons given off in the energy field and therefore the colors are really most visible against a white background. In the Philippines, there are several psychic surgeons who diagnose by observing the aura and who wrap their patients up in white sheets before they begin treatment. They do this because the aura becomes visible when reflected against the white sheet. Of course, it becomes confusing if the subject is standing directly in front of the light, as in front of a window, because then you do not know whether the light you see is shining from behind or whether it is a part of the person's energy field. In most cases, when people begin to see the energy fields around humans, they see the physical area first because it is the densest generally.

The next step is to start seeing rays because rays are more intense. Then they start seeing the auric field. It makes sense that the brighter colors would be seen first with the subtle colors falling away into nothingness. When people say you've got a yellow aura, what they might actually be seeing is the rain in such cases, they see it around the head and shoulders, but never below. When people come to the point where they can actually see are as well and are ready to begin interpreting them, I like to caution them about a few things, some of which I have said repeatedly in this book. First, we must realize that we're always looking through our own hours and we must know our are as well in order to be able to distinguish them from what we see in the energy fields of others. Second, it is a good idea to inform the other person that we are not observing the aura as it occurs objectively in its full and true nature, but that what we're observing of that person's aura depends on our state of consciousness at that moment. Third, we should never tell people they have lived their lives wrong because they have not used the properties of the energy we have observed.

We can only tell them what that energy is, mentioning the pros and cons and the areas where they may be vulnerable. Your disciplined practice may have improved your eyesight so that you are able to observe the brain, the aura, but that definitely does not put you in a position to tell anyone else what to do or not to do.

Chapter - 26

Five, the naturopathic system of energy regulation. Motion, the law of life. The basic law of life is motion, the rhythmic, cyclic pulsation of radiant energy, not only as radiant energy found in the universe at large, but it is characteristic of all living things and of each of us individually. This is not a vague, invisible force out there in the cosmos. It is very real and tangible, but it exists in our bodies, in our clothing and in the food we eat. Science is now discovering the matter itself is made up of this energy that beyond the molecule, beyond the atom, beyond the proton, the neutron and the electron, there are components that can no longer be characterized as matter, but can be considered either waves or particles, depending on the conditions under which they are observed. So from the viewpoint of quantum theory, all matter can be seen as a constant dance of energy, every particle of which we are composed is made up of these packets of radiant energy in constant motion.

Energy exists in four radical states, light, heat, moisture and crystallization. We do not have to delve very far into esoteric writings to realize that these radical states of energy correspond to the four elements of the ancient air, fire, water and earth. Each of these states exhibits a different mode of energy flow, ranging from swift to slow, from free to bound, but all of them are nevertheless characterized by energy in constant motion. Even the densest matter, such as metal or stone, is in constant, energetic motion. Because the human body participates in this universal movement of energy before radical energy, states must also be in evidence in the body. Indeed, the human body is designed for the transformation of energy from its pure form as light to its more solid, imprisoned form as fire, and then through electrochemical transformations into increasingly dense forms of liquids and solids, and through a reversal of this process of cannibalism and elimination, solids are once again transformed into liquid fire and light. Health as energy flow in order for energy to be transformed from one state to another, it must be in a constant flow through the body. We saw in Chapter one that the chakras or energy centers are the dynamos that provide the impetus for this flow.

When a Chalkias function is impeded or stagnated, this condition will be reflected in a decrease or distortion of its radiant output in the aura. Any density in our makeup will hamper the flow of energy among our molecules, one way of looking at illness is to characterize it as stagnant energy, energy that is not being heightened and transformed. We might compare our energy flow to the motion of a pendulum at each end of the pendulum swing; it has accumulated the kinetic power it needs to move back in the opposite direction. What happens when we hold on to energy? Let us say that one pull of the pendulum swing is labeled positive and the other negative. If we swing to the positive side and hold on to it, we're acting like goody goodies who refuse to look at the negative because we think anything negative is bad. If we hold on to the positive side, we can never swing to the negative and the energy of the pendulum becomes stagnant. There are other people who are going on to the negative and the same thing happens, the pendulum never reaches the positive anymore. So there's an erratic rhythm. In your body, that means there is stagnation somewhere of the energies within you in a healthy, active rhythm, the positive and negative are in a perfectly balanced state, which biologists call homeostasis. Ideally, we can go beyond the state of homeostasis.

We do not really need to watch if things are positive or negative, whether our condition is hyper or hypo. When people are in such a rhythm, there's no positive or negative anymore, just a perpetual mobile rhythm. Thus, the ideal is to achieve perpetual motion so that you do not need to think about positive and negative any longer, as long as we still have to bring the positive together with the negative. We are actually trying to create a current. Once the current has been achieved, if you just let it go from then on and keep operating in that bound state, you do not need to think in terms of positive and negative. A healthy body is one whose elements are in balance. We have said that radiant energy is the basic building block of our bodies as it is of the universe. This radiant energy which pervades all matter tens of itself to preserve its environment in balance and harmony through the principle of resonance. Is characteristic of this energy that it is progressive and evolutionary. Pulsating from one state to the next. Sickness occurs when we inhibit this pulse, restoring our energy and creatively and resist the transitions through the natural stages of our lives. It is not always obvious what these natural stages are, but we can begin to attend to a proper perspective when we realize that we cannot be alive and grow unless we can also die.

Fear plays a large part in illness, fear of dying, of leaving behind one stage and entering the next. This year restricts our flow of energy and stalls our growth. Our bodies are going through continuous changes every fraction of a second all during our lifetimes. These changes involve transformations and this process of transformation, which is life, is also a process of dying. An important aspect of balanced living, then, is balance time. As we take time out to eat and rest, we also need to take time out to die to encourage the progressive transition of ourselves through the stages of life. This time out for dying is how I think of meditation, that is the reason why the present volume on health follows the volume on meditation. Meditation is the basic initiator of all action. Every emotional and mental action thought immediately flows into physiological action. Thus, it is inevitable that heightened self awareness will influence the body and will affect important changes on the physical level.

It is only after we understand how these subtle influences can help us to maintain our health that we can truly understand the role of material aid in the process of preparing the body to heal itself. Assimilation through resonance. One way of looking at the mind body spectrum is to say that energy is expressed in two formats as pure energy or spirit and as matter. Pure energy is concerned with the causal side of our nature and matter Spirit's material form of expression. These two states of energy are very closely related, which helps to explain how some few individuals have been able to sustain their bodies on very rarefied nourishment, on energy. And it's merely a pure state. If through discipline and concentration, we were allowed our minds to operate fully in our bodies, we would still raise our transformational intensities so that we can be nourished by more and more subtle forms of energy, leaving behind food as we know it all together. Indents, earthly forms, magnetism is a force whereby opposites attract that are positive, attract negative, but in the more rarefied realm of pure spirit or mind, like attracts like. If we keep the body as radiant as possible, our higher consciousness will attract energy at that same high level and so we will avoid diseases.

On this high level of energy, which I call the power of magnetic, if we wait it out with a certain frequency of energy and with a certain amplitude, this will produce resonance with similar energies in the environment. Resonance is reprobation if I strike it on a violin and there is a piano three rooms away, that Gina will travel through the air and set up a resonant vibration in the G string of the piano, which will then reverberate in audibly back to the violin. The same thing is true of electromagnetic vibrations, which also have the capacity to resonate. Remember that all the particles you have in your body are also contained in the environment. Every particle has a capacity to produce an energetic outflow. Through this radiation coming from our bodies, then we attract those particles that are equal in the frequency and amplitude of their vibration. Most diseases can be characterized along a spectrum of sympathy and empathy. Sympathetic type people live on an emotional level, they resonate only with dense and low pulsations, attracting energy that stagnates in their gut, thus causing disease.

Empathy transforms this absorbed energy into a finer form, into light, and as it raises the amplitude of the energy, it will radiate out and be emitted rather than stagnating. For example, arthritis is a form of sympathetic illness. Arthritis in the body is usually matched by a rigid thinking in the mind, and the latter is often the cause of the former. To cure arthritis requires that the body and the mind both become more flexible. Injections can sometimes increase physical flexibility. But such treatment should be accompanied by mental relaxation as well. Obesity is also due to sympathy or overweight people are sponges for everyone else's problems, for their random, stagnant energy once absorbed, this energy settles in obese persons and does not move out again. Correspondingly, thoughts and feelings that do not get expressed and used will alter the body's chemistry, become dense and turn into fat. Sympathy means similar feelings, but empathy means energy and emotion . One secret of health is to raise gut feelings from the solar plexus level into the heart where they can be transformed and expressed, radiated outward. It is interesting that people who are thinkers and worriers are very sensitive to their environment.

Also attract the sympathetic feelings and energies out of their environment, quite often attract all kinds of particles to their bodies that become toxic to them. For example, we might look at numerous cases of skin condition, such as eczema, which dermatologists quite often have a very difficult time treating. They give the patients all kinds of tests and cannot find the cause of the skin condition, they may finally throw up their hands and say the skin problem is psychosomatic. I was treating a nine year old girl who would have an absolutely clear complexion when she went to school in the morning, she would be in class for half an hour. And if somebody in the class had a headache or a sore toe or a sore throat within that half an hour's time, the girl would have it too. The way she then tried to get rid of us by creating a poisonous substance in her body, which would cause her whole body to break out suddenly in eczema.

She had to be taught to have her energy flowing before she went to school so that she would have a good electrical field around her and would not pick up any of the lower things in our environment. These lower energies and toxic substances are all around this, but the only way we can be attracted to them is if we become electromagnetically sympathetic to them, if we let our energy go down. Doctors, Of course, refer to this condition as having a low resistance level. They should also call it a low consciousness level because consciousness means energy. When you expand your consciousness, you're expanding your energy. If you have a low resistance because you have a low consciousness, your immunity factor goes downhill. Note that the immunity mechanism is centered in the thymus gland, which is the gland associated with the heart chakra, the seat of consciousness. This is why you have to find excitement, enjoying all the things you do.

You can create this excitement within you, it is very valuable to realize that you can even use anger to create this excitement if you do not allow the anger to clot up in your solar plexus, where it will start to backfire on you. When you get angry, express emotion in a creative act, not by boxing your children in the ears. You can clean out your closet or your desk, shine your shoes or brush your clothes, dig in your garden. You may be muttering about that so and so the whole time, but if you use that anger, the energy will then be beneficial for you. It is not wasted and it does not affect you in the solar plexus area. Rather, it creates an energy field around you. This is a very important chapter for our modern world in which we are subjected to so many sources of frustration and anger. Some yogis use this tool when they go out into the desert and have nothing to get angry about anymore, but need extra energy for their meditation. They may see a fly or some other insect buzzing around them, and they appear to get terribly mad yelling, What is this insect doing in my environment?

I'm going to catch it. Through all their excitement, they suddenly feel charged up by the power and they go into meditation with new energy. Society has taught us that we must control our anger, but we have never understood the meaning of control. We always think of control as suppression or repression rather than as letting the energy flow. Power, which is another word for control, is a very valuable thing, but we use it wrongly, if not to repress ourselves, than to repress the rest of the world with it. So if you have anger, do not repress it, but bring it out in a powerful action, that does not mean you have to knock somebody over. There are plenty of things that need to be done that you can do with the energy from your anger. What I'm saying is that the energy we radiate is crucial in determining what we attract ourselves to. This principle of resinous underlies the approach I take to healing and nutrition.

Chapter - 27

Every particle of matter vibrates at a certain rate peculiar to itself through the process of assimilation, the body attracts to itself the elements it needs to grow and survive. The world around us contains all the nutrients we require for a healthy and balanced life. Quite often we do not choose what is suitable for our growth and balance maintenance, but even if we were to eat the right foods, we might still remain unhealthy because of poor assimilation. Chemical, nutritional or vitamin deficiencies, whatever you might call such causes of ill health, cannot be overcome merely by filling the organism with all of its missing elements and nutrients.

If the organism is not capable of absorbing these AIDS, it cannot regain balanced functioning, which is health. The body ingests nourishment in a heavy form because the body is heavy, a more subtle body stimulates finer energy, but the body has the potential and the task of transforming the energy it ingests into more subtle energy. We're not bound to the heaviness of our organisms, for we have the capacity to transform the energy within ourselves into finer and finer levels. We assimilate our nourishment from meat and spinach and eggs because we already share an affinity for the energy in these substances when they're assimilated into our organism. These substances assume a finer form and are put to more subtle uses. Assimilation is just another word for a resonance. The body assimilates more effectively as it resonates in rhythm with the more subtle, energetic pulses of the universe. This is our natural birth, right, and so we are responsible for the abuses, right, and cut ourselves off from the finer nourishment or energy surrounding this.

The proper approach to nutrition starts when we analyze our deficiencies and then prepare the body to satisfy its needs naturally from the world around it. The atmosphere and a reasonable doubt are enough to provide all our needs if the body is working at peak efficiency. You should not need to take vitamin or mineral supplements all your life, once an imbalance is identified, the body can be prepared to assimilate its needs and then given these needs in the form of a dietary supplement. Thereafter, the body can recover its own balance and maintain itself in health with no further external assistance. Let us now see how the body maintains this balance and how we prepare ourselves organically for autonomous health. I do electromagnetic energy regulation. We have already said that through electro chemical reactions within the body, there is a continuous transformation from chemistry into energy and from energy back into chemistry. How does this energy become available to the body and how does it undergo such transmutations?

The exchange of energy in our bodies takes place through the exchange of ions, which are simply components of molecules, other atoms or groups of atoms that have lost or taken on electrons and hence have an electric charge. The molecules of which our bodies are composed are actually built up and broken down through the exchange of ions, the affinities that unite these two spheres of life, the ionic and the molecular, are really only extensions of that invisible activity that pervades the universe. The electromagnetic force is radiating in all directions. Our bodies are composed for the most part of water, the processes of this mass of water which flows through our body are of the utmost importance because the body fluids act as a catalyst, carrying and adjusting all external influences and nutrition throughout every part of the body. Furthermore, the power of magnetic quality of body fluids, like attraction, depends on a constant process of the creation and combination of ions in this fluid on the ionic balance between positive and negative. To make changes in the body then means to change the electromagnetic state of the body's fluid, electricity is the particular characteristic of the energy force we're dealing with, and magnetism is the direction given to that force.

Disease, old age and other alterations in the body's energy patterns are ultimately traceable to imbalances and declines in the electrical potency of the body's plasma. It's an intermolecular fluid. In its function as a catalyst, it is important that our body fluid conducts electrochemical energy in just the right way. If our water were just a conductor, pure and simple, that would mean that any electrical energy contained in it would be dissipated, distributed out. A good conductor without insulation cannot retain any energy in it, and the energy in such a fluid would simply disappear over a period of time. Our body fluid must be electric, chemically balanced, so that it can conduct energy without losing it. It should be water. Distilled water is perfectly neutral in this sense, which means that it can latch onto all chemicals and nutrients and charges and retain them. In this connection, we might look at the current popularity of waterbeds.

People get very excited about sleeping in waterbeds, but they often complain that they're terribly tired. They do not realize that they have opened all the gates of their energies because the water in the water bed is tap water, which is so chemically unbalanced that it is conductive, meaning that all the energies go through it and dissipate. All the psychic energy, all the thought patterns, all the electrical messages, everything moves through the water and is lost. This may affect your mental state, you may have terrible subconscious dreams on a waterbed because there is no isolation and you start to let your own energy leak out. This condition is what I call a bleeding, or it can also result from a lack of the proper electrochemical insulation in the body's fluids, and it is elements such as calcium that provide this insulation in our bodies. So if you want to sleep on a waterbed, that is fine. As long as you go to the extra trouble and expense of filling it with distilled water, then it is not conductive anymore. It is dielectric. Then your energies will not be dissipated during the night elements and sell salts.

The basic chemical elements are those substances. We need to be healthy. In the normal growth fashion in which our bodies function, we derive nourishment from energy and molecular form or food. What the body is really doing to obtain nourishment is to assimilate the basic ionic vibrations of the particular elements that it needs and that exist in various foods. My program of health and nutrition is therefore concerned with bringing the body into a state in which it is able to assimilate, break down and extract the nutrition it requires. Let me provide an example of assimilation. If my body needs the elements, can I eat a cucumber which contains silicone? But how can Brazil get assimilated by my body's fluid substance, which is where the silicon will be most effective. Absorption is not certain enough for absorption refers only to the molecular process, and now that we know we must focus on the ionic level, we want to encourage another process, which is resonance.

Like, attracts like and ironic electromagnetism, so attraction and assimilation are accomplished when the ironic resonance of silicon is matched by resonance of the body fluid. But the body fluid will only radiate with the pulse of silicon when the fluid already contains enough of the elements silicon to make it so resonant. That is. If the body fluid is to extract the silicone contained in the cucumber, there have to be silicone oils already in the body fluid. So if there is a serious silicone deficiency in the body, eating cucumbers will not solve it because the body cannot properly assimilate it. The assaults of which there is a 12 hour special class of homeopathic, we prepared chemical compounds, each consisting of an electro positive and an electronegative component or iron that I've been subjected to a very special process of dilution to make these elements more readily available to the body. This employment of elements in combination, such as sodium with phosphorus is designed to anticipate the body's mode of attracting what is required. Of sodium or phosphorus. In the case of these two elements, for example, the phosphorus is in the form of phosphate, in isolation as pure elements, the sodium and the phosphorus may be difficult to assimilate, but in order to be combined into assault, they must already be in ironic form and thus they help each other to be assimilated. If the body requires an energy supplement, it will not do any good to stuff the organism with only a positively charged ion.

The body. As a bipolar electrical energy field requires both parties to be activated, so an energy supplement should contain both a positively charged element such as Iren and an equal amount of a negatively charged element such as phosphorus. These nutrients can be put into the organism in the form in which they have been stimulated by other living things in plants and animal tissues, rich in iron and phosphorus or in a diluted form in a cell salt. The salt salts are so named because they represent levels of dilution approaching the concentration of these substances in the cells themselves. When I say the summersaults are deluded, I do not necessarily mean they are watered down. On the contrary, a high energy is obtained through dilution in the preparation of cell salts, the dilution process consists of repeated duration, which is the painstaking grinding of the chemical compound, or salt in a mortar and pestle, together with a substance that is electro chemically neutral and that is capable of taking the impression of the electrically charged ions of the salt, insulating it and holding it.

Lactose or milk sugar is such a substance, it will retain the electrical potential of the cell salt until it is released by being put into a fluid. This is the reason for never taking cells so diluted in water or even in the hand, as soon as they come into contact with moisture, they lose their charge or potency before they have a chance to enter the body. The process of iteration is a process of serial dilution of the salts with lactose in the ratio of one part of the salt to nine parts of lactose or a one to 10 dilution. After the original one to 10, dilution has been meticulously prepared by long grinding together of the substances, one part of this mixture is traded with another nine parts of lactose to produce a one to one hundred dilution. The process is repeated until the desired dilution or potency is obtained. Carmen Potencies, Fassel salts are three times, which means one part in 10 to the power of three or one in one thousand six times or 10 to the power of six, which is equal to one to one million and 12 times or 10 to the power of 12, which is the same as a one to one billion dilution. This does not mean that the less diluted form or lower potency is necessarily stronger, less diluted also means denser, and the denser the material, the longer it takes to be assimilated, whereas the more diluted form is more quickly assimilated and the stairs up the system more.

Those are the three times strength, a relatively low potency or low dilution is suitable for slow building up as it magnesium phosphate when a higher potency or higher dilution might be too much of a shock to the system, where six times is appropriate for instances in which prompt action is necessary. Where the south salt of anabolic or building up processes in the body, the elements control the catabolic or breaking down processes. Together, these processes constitute metabolism, so metabolism is really an expression of the dual active conservation and distribution of vital energy throughout the body, which are the work of the cell salts and the elements. Many minerals and trace elements are the specific forms in which the four basic elements of the ancients are found on the planet.

Despite their sometimes dense appearance, the elements all function within living organisms to encourage the movement or distribution of energy. Trace elements are so-called because only the merest traces of these substances are found throughout the body and especially in the glands associated with the seven chakras. The minerals, in contrast, are found in relatively large quantities, some of them are among the basic building blocks of the body. However, whether the minerals and trace elements exist in large or infinitesimally small quantities in the body, they all appear to be vital to the maintenance of the healthy, balanced, functioning of the organism. Although our bodies contain aspects of all the organic life forms on our planet, they are also unable to exist without inorganic foundations, the elements. All organic processes are bound up with the inorganic activities in the soil, which holds in balance the relationship between the salts and the elements. Those assaults represent the usual structures that condense, insulate and transmit the ionized potency of the basic elements from their raw state through the body's digestive process and finally into the body fluid. This assault thus aiding the distribution of the elements throughout the body. So salts are compounds, and like all chemical compounds, they represent imprisoned potential energy awaiting release.

The purpose of cell salts is to produce stability by integrating and utilizing the energies of the elements through centripetal or inward drawing forces. In contrast, the elements are the centrifugal or outward moving forces that distribute radiant energy throughout the body in waves and whirls, horizontal and vertical waves. These great vortices, the radiant patterns that, as we have seen, are the characteristic features of the aura. The ions of dissolved salts regulate metabolism, and in this way, the salts balance the centrifugal radiance of the elements. This balance is very tenuous. The slightest imbalance in the fluid chemistry will have wide repercussions in the entire organism. The minerals and trace elements must be in proper balance in our bodies.

Chapter - 28

If they are to fulfill their role of distributing energy. If they're out of balance, they are not able to trigger the energy and keep it flowing. For example, if a person has a potassium deficiency, there's automatically also excessive sodium content in their body. Such an imbalance is like a short circuit in our energy pattern. That is why we need to address such imbalances by the use of cell salts. Table three lists some of the important elements and minerals in their three states, each of these elements has a certain set of qualities and is associated with a certain wavelength.

This is the basis for what I call the selective affinities to which I refer in Chapter six, when these elements are combined with each other to form assault, the resulting compound has new characteristics that may differ from the original elements. Table three describes the elements in their three states, along with what makes each of them important for the body. The description of a cell sold in Table four may be quite different from those of two elements of which it is formed. Table three, some important minerals and trace elements. Element, calcium, electric charge, electric positive or alkaline forming? Description and function and metallic substance found in alkaline earth, such as lime and chalk, a base for plaster of Paris calcium solidifies and crystallizes and therefore acts as an integrator, a building block for the nervous system. It acts as an insulator. Its utility is not limited to the bones.

Calcification in the body can be broken up with calcium and ionic form, which will spread the calcium to other parts of the body. Therefore, breaking up calcium crystallization. Organs requiring calcium are adrenal cortex, muscles, nails, ovaries, prostate, skeleton, skin, teeth and thymus. Dietary sources of calcium are Armin's Brazil nuts, citrus peel, filbert nuts, green vegetables, leaves of herbs and plants, milk, seaweed, sesame seeds and sunflower seeds. The element of chlorine has an electric charge of electronegative, it is acid forming. Its description and function are a greenish yellow gas two and a half times heavier than air and very soluble in water, so it is fast acting and solution, poisonous in gas form, essential for the formation of hydrochloric acid, releasing oxygen in the process. Hydrochloric acid is needed for digestion and for the brain. Organs requiring chloride are hair, intestines, liver muscles, pancreas, skin, spleen, teeth and thyroid, there are two sources of corn are avocado, celery, coconut dates, kale, kelp, lettuce, tomato and turnip.

The element copper has an electric charge of electric positive, it is alkaline forming, its description and function are a reddish brown, malleable and ductile metal that is an excellent conductor of electricity and heat. Essential for utilization of iron in the diet, highly concentrated in pineal gland, however, too much copper can make you sluggish. Organs requiring copper or blood, brain, liver and pancreas. Does your source of copper affricate beans, especially pinto beans, nuts and whole grains? The element flooring is electronegative or acid forming its description and function are a yellowish green gas, corrosive, poisonous, the most highly reactive element known a toxin destroys organic substances and excess can cause spinal and bone diseases. Organs requiring fluoride are adrenal cortex, brain eye's ovaries, prostate, teeth and thymus. Dietary sources of fluoride are almonds, beet greens, carrots, dandelion greens, spinach and greens. The element iodized is electronegative or acid forming. Its description and function are a non metallic element in the same family as chlorine and fluorine consisting of grayish black volatile crystals that form a violet colored vapor essential to the synthesis of thyroid hormones, deficiency can lead to greater. Organs requiring iodine, our adrenal medulla hair, pituitary and thyroid.

Dietary sources of iodine are asparagus, blueberries, dulce, Irish moss, kale, kelp, all seafood, especially shellfish, spinach, Swiss chard, turnip greens and watermelon. The ultimate irony is neutral or catalyst, its description and function appears in nature as a metallic or that is a mineral mixed with a metal from which the metal is extracted. It is essential for the formation of hemoglobin and in combination with potassium, it is a carrier of oxygen and an excellent healing agent as iron phosphate, it can raise blood pressure so must be used with caution. Organs requiring iron are adrenal cortex, blood, brain, heart, kidneys, muscles, ovaries, prostate, skin and thymus.

Dietary sources of ironer, cayenne pepper, dulce green vegetable leaves, kelp squash wines, port and sherry wines are a suitable way for older persons to acquire easily assimilated Iren. Element, magnesium. It is electron positive or alkaline forming, its description of function are. A silver white metal, hard and light, it burns very bright. The general distributor of other elements in the organism restores the current of the energy and blood and nerves. The efficiency may cause weakness, depression, disturbances and muscle contraction. Organs requiring magnesium are adrenals, brain, intestines, kidneys, liver, pancreas, spleen and thyroid. There are three sources of magnesium: almonds, bananas, beans, dates, dried fruit, all green kelp and potatoes. The element, manganese is neutral or catalyst. Is description and function, a grayish white metal, usually hard and brittle rust like iron, but is not magnetic organs requiring manganese.

Our adrenal medulla brain is pineal and pituitary. Dietary sources of manganese are beets, carrots, celery, chives, cucumbers and parsley. That element phosphorus is electronegative or acid forming is description and function are a white and waxy solid, becoming yellow when exposed to light, when exposed to air, it gives off white fumes and an odor of garlic. It can be very poisonous, but as an ingredient of myelin, it acts as a protective agent for muscular tissue and for nerve AIDS in the proper assimilation of calcium and magnesium. Organs requiring phosphorus are adrenal medulla, brain, part, hair and pituitary. Dietary sources for phosphorus are beans, dried fruit, all grains, green vegetable leaves, nuts, seaweed and all seeds. Potassium has an electrical charge of electric positive or alkaline forming. Its description and function are a silver white substance that easily unites with oxygen, it decomposes in water, producing a slight explosion and flame.

Crucial in maintaining balance in the nervous system, in each nerve cell, the center should be filled with potassium ions, the membrane with sodium ions and the structure solidified with calcium and silicon. Also produces and regulates body heat. Organs required are heart, liver muscles, pancreas, spleen, stomach and digestive tract and thyroid. Dietary sources are avocado, bananas, beans, beets, carrots, dried fruit and vegetable leaves, nuts, radishes and seaweed. The element silicon has an electric charge of electronegative or acid forming.

Description functions are found in rock crystals such as quartz and Flint, a very hard substance fowling mineral springs; it not only promotes firmness and strength in the organism, but also radiates energy. It can form itself into a wide variety of crystal forms, such as acid eats away the calcium covering the bones, liver oils where re lubricate dried bones and silicon as an LSD Cizre with calcium will restore bones. Healing properties, integrated, stabilizes, cuts away, Percheron matter. Organs require our adrenal cortex, brain eye's hair, heart, ovaries, prostate, skin, teeth and thymus. Dietary sources are avocado, cucumbers, dandelions, lettuce, shaved grass, strawberries and sunflower seeds. The element sodium has an electric charge of electron positive or alkaline forming. Its description and function are a soft, silvery white, waxy metallic substance, it has a great affinity for water. It floats on the surface and gradually disappears with a hissing noise indicating that hydrogen is being given off, forming caustic soda.

All sodium should be kept well sealed to prevent access to air predominant and intracellular fluid in excess can cause edema. Organs require our gallbladder, intestines, liver, nails, pancreas, skeleton, skin, spleen, stomach, and they just have checked teeth and thyroid. That source is beets, carrots, celery, dried fruit, kale, kelp, radishes and raisins. Delmon Sulfur has an electric charge of Electronegative. Its description and function are a solid crystal, greenish gray with a faint odor and taste, although it fuses and boils, it is insoluble in water. It burns with a blue flame when united with oxygen. Organs requiring our adrenal medulla eyes, hair, nails, pituitary skeleton, skin, stomach and digestive tract and teeth. Dietary sources are kale, kelp, lettuce, raspberries and turnips. The element zinc has an electric charge of electron positive or alkaline forming its description and function are a bluish white metal, highly concentrated in the gland organs requiring our hair.

Dietary sources are celery, lettuce, sunflower seeds, wheat germ. Instructions for taking cell salts, the purpose of maintaining the proper cell salt balance in the body is to attract and extract the mineral elements we need from our regular diet. Under ordinary circumstances, the cell salts themselves should also be readily extracted from our diet. But to counteract specific deficiencies, it is appropriate to stimulate the process of assimilation by taking the extracted cell salts in tablet form. Because cell phones are among the least potentially detrimental dietary supplements you can take, it is safe to experiment on yourself with them. After analyzing your needs and possible deficiencies by studying

Table four and also perhaps following the suggestions for your tarot card, you may select one or more cell sources to try. A normal dosage would be 16 tablets per day in four tablets, four times during the day, or eight tablets twice a day in the morning and in the evening. Because these salts have an electrical potential, it is very important to take them dry with a spoon and never to touch them with your hands.

The moisture in your skin is ionized and will neutralize the potency of the tablets. That is your own body moisture would literally charge to sell salts. You can also just pour the indicated number of tablets into the bottle cap and then directly into your mouth. As I noted earlier, never take the tablets with water, just let them dissolve under your tongue. Keep the bottle tightly closed and away from moisture, heat, light and other medicinal substances. If you begin taking a specific cell assault for a specific ailment, do so for a few months and then stop. The body should have been able in that time to make up its deficiency and you should see some improvement in your body's ability to assimilate its requirements, as evidenced by lessening of your deficiency symptoms. Thereafter, you may take bioplasma, which is a balanced maintenance combination of self salts, if you see no improvement in your condition after taking the cell salt, you will need to analyze your eating habits and your way of living more carefully to ascertain what may be preventing the South salt treatment from taking effect. A survey of South Salt.

The three principal electric positive elements that are attracted to the body and from which to sell salts are formed are sodium, potassium and calcium. Sodium or Natrium has a strong affinity for water, and so it is a potent distributor of fluids throughout the body. Potassium or calcium has a tendency to unite with oxygen, to produce heat and fire, and so it is an important element in producing and regulating body temperature. Calcium or Casoria has the chief properties of integration, solidification and crystallization. It is therefore an important building block of body tissues. The sell salts may be organized into four biotech classes based on their function within the group as follows: shifting or sulfur group. This group stirs up and shifts waste matter, eating detoxification, it includes sodium sulfate, potassium sulfate and calcium sulfate eliminating or chlorine group. This group encourages efficient elimination of putrid matter.

This recuperative function suitably follows the cleansing function of the first group. This group includes sodium chloride, potassium chloride and sodium phosphate. Binding or calcium group? This group promotes integration of matter and the building up of new matter. It includes calcium sulfate, calcium fluoride and iron phosphate distributing or phosphorus group. This group, which controls molecular balance and the rhythms of the healthy organism, includes potassium, phosphate, magnesium, phosphate and silica. Table four indicates the principle function of each of the cell salts, as well as conditions that may indicate a deficiency or imbalance of that cell in the body, on the basis of these descriptions, you may be able to ascertain which of the cell salts you may need to restore a healthy balance in the functioning of your body. Table for selling salts.

Sulphur or shifting group? Calcium phosphate. This also acts like water in the body, integrating all the body's tissues, it is found in all the tissues of the body is essential to the sound formation of bone and proper growth. And is a vital element in all the functions of nutrition and assimilation. Checks, dehydration and violent elimination processes, control solidifying activities and prevent them from becoming extreme deficiency conditions include bone diseases, defective nutrition, poor teeth weakness, M.S., Asian digestive disturbances, slow growth in children, delayed teething. A general nutrient for simple anemia, debility and impaired digestion, especially vulnerable in old people for its restorative powers after acute illness. Potassium sulfate. Promotes the formation of oils and the body softens and lubricates tissues, breaks up solid deposits, keeps the pores open, ejects oil and encourages perspiration. This all has a great affinity for the skin and mucous membranes, acting both as a lubricant and as a healer through its promotion of Oscar Grecians.

Good for minor skin eruptions, bronchial khattar. Abuses of the balance of this cell assault are characterized by yellowish, slimy secretions, yellow coated tongue, indigestion secretions from eyes, ears and nose with characteristic yellowish color. Also, it is excellent for calcium deposits in combination with silica. Sodium sulfate, this salt is not a constituent of cells, it is found only in the intracellular fluid. It influences the expression of superfluous water by attracting and extracting fluid from the organism it stirs up and shifts body fluids during the process of digestion, elimination and respiration. For this reason, Nathuram Sopi is added to some degree to Reddick's. This is especially attractive to the intestinal and abdominal regions. It is excellent for serious conditions with such symptoms of greenish brown coated root of tongue, bitter taste, colic and so on for liver problems and to counter influenza. Chlorine or eliminating group potassium chloride distributes oxygen throughout the body, promoting oxygenation of the organism and thus assisting in the elimination of waste matter stirs up organic energy and awakens dormant life. Forces act as an antidepressant as it creates and moves, energy can create real explosions of energy.

The metabolic function of Collimore is to unite with a woman to form fibrin when this cell salt is not in proper balance. Albumin is released in the form of thick, white, sticky discharges from the skin or mucous membranes, white or gray coated. A good blood conditioner for use against cough, colds, respiratory ailments follows firm plus when excretions set, inform the affected parts. Sodium chloride. This is a constituent of every liquid and hands of every solid in the body. The body is about 70 percent water and naturally regulates the proper utilization of water and the degree of moisture in the cells. It attracts water from. Without taking moisture from the atmosphere and thereby helping the body to adapt to atmospheric changes. It also helps attract and stabilize fluids from foods. A deficiency of the salt may cause the water to remain in the intracellular fluids, leading to bloating and profuse watery secretions. Deficiency may also cause drowsiness and loss of smell and taste. Sodium phosphate regulates the alkaline acid balance of the body as an organizer. It decomposes and emulsifies fatty tissue useful in diets to prevent fat from settling in one place.

Also used as an acid mutualization for conditions of excessive acidity, digestive upsets, heartburn, yellowish itching secretions from skin or membranes, tongue with creamy yellow coating stomach and intestinal disturbances. Calcium.

Chapter - 29

Or a binding group, calcium fluoride. This assault is a constituent of the elastic fibers of the skin, connective tissue and blood vessels, as well as being found in the glands, bones and tooth enamel. It solidifies and crystallized fluids binding colonial substances, a non conductor of nerve energy, it isolates the nerve cells and helps protect the organism from overstrained it, vacated in conditions of dilated, relaxed blood vessels or elastic tissues such as varicose veins, impaired circulation, hemorrhoids, muscular weakness, heart or swollen glands prevents nails and hair from becoming brittle. Calcium sulfate salts function is to destroy worn out red blood cells, thereby promoting their elimination from the body.

Unless the body wrestles and is extremely absorbent, it absorbs disease cells and bacteria, covers and protects all soft tissues from deteriorating and injury. Impaired function of the cell salt will produce symptoms such as standing disorders, ulceration, Boyle's respiratory ailments, unhealthy skin, slow healing, minor injuries, thick yellowish offensive secretions. It is a blood purifier that will help clear up minor skin irritations, acne and pimples as its slow healing wounds. Iron phosphate, a constituent of the hemoglobin in red blood cells, the cells that controls the formation of hemoglobin and the distribution of oxygen through the body to the body. This combination of iron with phosphorus can raise blood pressure, so it must be taken with caution, a deficiency can produce symptoms of anemia leading to fever and inflammation and especially good cells to children, especially for sniffles, colds and anemia.

Indicated in the early stages of most ailments characterized by fever, inflammation, heat and pain, especially before secretions from the affected parts said. Phosphorus or distributing group, magnesium phosphate. This assault is composed of two light producing elements, magnesium, which is capable of spreading out in long, thin threads and which burns with a brilliant light and phosphorus which emits light spontaneously. Megaforce is essentially to the metabolic processes of the nerve and muscle fibers of the body. The light producing powers of its component elements make it an excellent distributor of energy throughout the body, its radiating qualities make it able to cut across fibers and disperse tangled knots of tension as abdominal plexi or the hypo gastric gland.

An excellent distributor of vital energy throughout the organism restores normal body rhythm. The efficiency of the salt is marked by muscular fiber contractions, painful spasms of the nerves and muscles, characteristic symptoms of deficiency are sharp, darting, spasmodic pains, neuralgic pains in any part of the body in various nerve disorders. The use of Megaforce, an alteration with Kelly force is usually very desirable. Potassium phosphate. A constituent of the tissues of nerves, brain and muscles, as well as of blood cells. This all combines the elements of air and fire. It stimulates the nerve fibers and awakens the protoplasm activity in the cells. This is the basic Sult for brain tissues and nerve fluids. It unclogs the flow of energy, giving a lively, tingling feeling to the body. It is the most radioactive of all the cell salts, as well as having a tendency to unite with carbon. This assault, which is lacking in many individuals, is a stimulating salt awakening the activity of the whole substantial self.

Deficiency symptoms include mental weaknesses, depression, irritability, nervousness, sometimes general debility, neuralgic pains. This assault is often used to counter nervous indigestion and nervous headache. Cilicia. This oxide of silicon is the only cell sort that is not a double salt composed of two mineral elements. So Ostia is an integral part of the structure of plants and to a lesser extent of animals and humans. It can issue a variety of crystalline formations and so imparts strength and integration to the body. It is a constituent of bones, joints, glands, skin and mucous surfaces. Celestial functions as an electrical insulator and purifies the system by controlling the normal molecular flow, keeping the organism in rhythmic balance, it gives firmness and vibrancy to the nerves and tissues. It exerts cleansing and healing action symptoms. Calling for Susya include Cafaro conditions of the respiratory organs with offensive pulse like charges, offensive characteristic secretions, skin eruptions with offensive discharges, spirit of conditions that are slow to heal, small wounds that are slow to heal.

An introduction to the use of Erb's. ERs are once again becoming an increasingly popular means of treating the illness, these medicinal plants not only act in a remedial manner, but also help to keep the energy flowing. Appendix, a list, many common medicinal herbs, and their therapeutic applications, medicinal herbs should not be taking daily maintenance basis. Rather, they should be used as specific remedies. When something goes wrong with your body, it is alright to drink tea as refreshing beverages. But in that case, avoid using the same herb all the time or you will get a medicinal effect. When I give herbs for medicinal purposes, I very rarely give single or rather I give them in combination, the most important herb in such a combination is the curative, which is the one that is selected for its medicinal effect on the specific condition being treated. This one created may have such a strong action on the body, that is it best to tone it down. That is why I give another or a demotion which softens the harshness of the creative.

I also gave aromatic tea, which imparts fragrance and flavor to the herbal tea. Sometimes I add a fourth R which serves as an activator or a tonic to reinforce to create the type of activator I personally prefer to give would be a laxative to make sure that we start removing some of the morbid matter through the intestinal tract. If you refer to Appendix, say, you will find that there are a number of herbs listed as Demosthenes since aromatics and laxatives, after you've selected the creative for the specific therapeutic action you need. You can then choose a most aromatic and laxative according to what you feel is suitable in each particular case. In preparing an herbal tea, the curative should be twice the dosage of the other herbs. If we say that half a teaspoon is equal to one part, then the creative would be two parts or one teaspoon. For one part of water, the component Erb's should be in the following proportions, curative, two parts equal to one teaspoon. You mustn't have one part equal to half teaspoon aromatic.

One part equals half tablespoon. Laxative optional, one part equals to half teaspoon. Unless you're directed, otherwise, you're listening for a particular verb, never boil your Erb's with the water. The few herbs that are boiled are the exception or the water first. As for regular tea, add the herbs in indicated proportions, steep the mixture for 10 to 15 minutes and 30 by a cup. You should not boil the ERBs with the water because you may begin to extract chemicals in the boiling process that will act unpredictably on you or will interact with each other. If you simply add freshly bottled water to the herbs, the heat of the boiled water will be sufficient to drop the medicinal ingredients. 10 to 15 minutes is just the amount of time it takes to draw up the medicinal virtues of the Earth's. To illustrate the use of Appendix A. and the formula for blended teas, let us say that you are suffering from nervousness and headache as a curative. You will want an herb for your nerves. So you look nervous. Blaring is a good choice as a Norvan. So you can use one teaspoon of valerian as a curative.

Now you must select a demo and aromatic and optionally a laxative. There's no particular pattern to these supplementary verbs, for example, certain aromatics do not necessarily go with certain creative's. This is a matter of personal taste. But if you can find an aromatic or a mouse that has the same application as a creative as well as its supplementary function, then you would pick such an IRB to help the creative chapter. When you look under aromatics, for example, you will find camomile checking under Camomile in part two of Appendix A, you will find the caramel is an agent as well as an aromatic. It is logical then that you would prefer Camomile as an aromatic one that has nothing to do with calming the nerves. But it is up to you to make the choice. It is not really that important. You may find then that an IRB fills a double function if your purpose is to get rid of a headache and calm your nerves. You have a double effect from Camomile as an aromatic because it also reinforces the combative action of the Valaria.

We needed them also to licorice root is listed under Demosthenes in part one, but in part two you will find that it is also a laxative. It would make no sense then in this particular case, to add a fourth or. The licorice root can function both as a mouse and as a laxative. Our recipe for the herbal tea for nervousness and headache would then be one quart water boiled, one teaspoon valerian root, curative, half teaspoon camomile aromatic half teaspoon licorice root the mustn't and laxative. Boil water to the ORMs Steve for 10 to 15 minutes and drink one cup at a time. People also use Irv's as flavoring agents in cooking, there is no reason why you should not do this, Of course, but be prepared for any medicinal effects such as herbs may have. For example, you can make a nice licorice ice cream or licorice pudding. What if you put a lot of licorice roots in your food? Do not be surprised if you find yourself making a lot of trips to the bathroom. Licorice can be a very strong laxative. So you would never think of using and cooking because they have a bad taste, for example, you would never put valerian root in the salad because it has a nasty, bitter taste. This is a reason we use aromatic and herbal teas to take away the harshness of the flavor of the creative to make it more palatable.

This brief introduction should enable you to make use of the information on Irv's in appendix, a one warning is in order. Note that some verbs are marked with asterisks. As noted in the introduction to Appendix A, these herbs are toxic in one way or another and should be avoided if possible. In any case, they should only be used under the conditions described in the introduction to the appendix. Some observations on diet, the elements from the earth's crust are an excellent source of energy. Table three, describe some dietary sources of important minerals and trace elements. Remember, however, that your body must be able to assimilate these elements from your food if your diet is to do you any good. Therefore, if you're eating the proper balanced diet and still show deficiency symptoms, you might look into the use of cell salts to prepare your body to assimilate nutrients properly. In general, root vegetables have a much higher mineral and trace element content than plants that grow above the soil. Red beets, for example, are a tremendous source of energy plants grown in volcanic soil, and seaweeds such as dulse and kelp are also very rich sources of nutrients.

For those people who want to avoid eating meat, a vegetarian diet is perfectly capable of providing the body with its nutrients. But one must remember to diversify the vegetarian cuisine with plenty of non green vegetables. Sometimes vegetarians look lethargic and mentally dull, which may be because they're taking in excessive quantities of green vegetables, which have a tendency to relax and dull the organism. Why energy is much more concentrated in pigments and vegetables, such as red cabbage, beets, parsnips, radishes and carrots. In salads, a good proportion is 70 percent pigmented vegetables to 30 percent greens. Of course, this suggestion depends on the kind of activity a person engages in his or her daily life. It is important to discharge as much energy as you're absorbing if you engage in a great deal of physical and mental exertion as a matter of routine. There is little danger that you will consume more meat and or pigmented vegetables than you burn up. On the other hand, a person who has achieved a very subtle state, which would be the only healthy reason for not engaging in a great deal of physical and mental exertion, is functioning with very fine energy and does not require meat or pigmented vegetables.

Many people are very inactive, both physically and creatively. The cure, Of course, is to change one's routine. But until one has done so, there's not much sense in taking a lot of vitamins, which the body cannot store if it has no need of them. Was there any reason to eat large quantities of meat and pigmented vegetables, this additional energy will not be discharged and it will only add to the organism's problem of stored up stagnating energy.

One brief note on the subject of vitamin supplements may be in order, why supplements will do you no good if you do not have sufficient trace elements in your body to activate them. It has been said that the urine of Americans is the most expensive urine in the world because it contains all the high priced vitamins that are ingested and cannot be utilized. The elements and the sells salts that are inorganic basis that are minimally required if vitamins are to be effective. So it is useless to take vitamins. If you neglect the balance of minerals and trace elements as we've seen, it may be necessary to take some salts to adjust your mineral balance until the body can stimulate these important elements for itself. Fasting. So investing damages the body more than it helps it, the body needs time to adjust to the new eating habits and therefore the best way to fast is to take thirty six days altogether, 12 days to build up to the fast 12 days during which you do not take in anything but water and 12 days to break the fast. During the first 12 days, there should be the following program of decreased food intake, first date, three quarters breakfast, lunch and dinner, second day, half breakfast, lunch and dinner, third day, one fourth of breakfast, lunch and dinner.

Fourth day, no breakfast, lunch and dinner. Fifth day, no breakfast. Three quarters of lunch and dinner. Six days. No breakfast. Half lunch and dinner. Seventh day. No breakfast. One fourth lunch and dinner. Eighth day, no breakfast, no lunch, dinner. Ninth day, no breakfast, no lunch, three fourths dinner. Tenth day, no breakfast, no lunch, have dinner, 11th day, no breakfast, no lunch and one fourth dinner, 12th day, no food except water. Twelve days, twenty fourth days, no food except water. Twenty fifth days to thirty six, they build back up to regular eating by starting to eat as on 11th day and reversing down today one then resuming full meals, taking responsibility for your health. Our discussion of the processes of nutrition and assimilation has made it clear that how you live has a tremendous impact on your physical health.

Health is not just the absence of disease, it is a dynamic evolutionary process, a state of constant change. You're made up of some three hundred and fifty trillion cells, each one unique and each with the capacity to maintain and reproduce itself and to interact and interrelate with all the other cells of the body. Every particle that makes up the components of the cell is in a state of constant activity and there is a constant flow of energy arising from that activity because health is equivalent to the free, unimpeded flow of energy. You can see that it is possible to interfere with your health to make yourself ill by intervening on the subtlest least material level. The bodies of this organism will keep functioning if you do not interfere with it. Volunteer control really means allowing the body to control itself by not attachment rather than by becoming attached to all things that are going on in the body by not thinking rather than by thinking that you know better than the body. Although, as we have seen, you're responsible for the state of your own health and also for your own healing, your mind by itself cannot sculpt out your own be your mind can only achieve its goals if the body is in a physiologically balanced state and then electromagnetically balanced condition.

Mind and body are interdependent, so as long as your body is not fully able to extract its energy needs autonomously from the outside, you will need to help it along by using cell salts, Irv's and the carefully adjusted diet. The immediate goal is to put the body back in balance so that you do not need to supplement it any longer. This will leave you free to focus on developing your mental and spiritual capacity to follow the purpose indicated by your ray. Your mind, like your body, will not attract the vibrations it needs for expansion unless it is already emitting the same vibration that it hopes to attract. When you're able to do this, then with your mind as a tool, you can do anything you want as long as the mind is part of a healthy body to carry out its decisions fully. Once you have begun to treat your physical problems with doses of the cell salts, which in turn will enable your body fluid to attract the elements it requires, then you must complement this process with a mental one just as you're expanding your body's ability to maintain its own balance. You must expand your mind and raise your overall energy level to emit subtler energy and thereby to attract more of it to yourself.

As you lower the frequency and increase the amplitude of the vibrations of your physical being and so heightened the voltage of your ionic recharged body fluid, you also automatically open up wider channels for expanded levels of consciousness. This is what we really mean when we talk about holistic medicine, a system of health maintenance that permits the free, unimpeded flow of energies, the expression of the potential of your whole self.

Chapter - 30

Six tarried systems of natural healing. In the preceding chapters of this book, we have discussed a number of approaches to health and the free expression of the abilities with which we were born. We have seen that such diverse approaches and meditation, the use of color and sound herbs, nutrients, salt and minerals can all help us to maintain the balance of physical, mental and spiritual expression that we define as health.

For some years now, I've been working with a system that integrates these diverse forms of therapy and health maintenance by identifying for each person a symbol derived from the terror attack that resonates with all the other health maintenance influences he or she needs to use. The system is not infallible, and I am by no means satisfied that I have exhausted all the possibilities yet, but I have found that this tiered system will give me an accurate picture of an individual, even if he or she is not present. Later, when I actually see the person, the perceptions I have arrived at through the system are generally confirmed and many of the person's characteristics can be seen to fit together. The origin of the twenty two cards of the major arcana. There is an anecdote in the arcane tradition that shortly before the capture of the ancient city of Alexandria and the burning of its famous library, the high priest devised a way of preserving their esoteric knowledge. They analyzed their wisdom and drove twenty two major mysteries and fifty six minor mysteries.

As a further security, these Seventy-eight mysteries were translated into images that ultimately became the seventy eight cards of the deck. The story goes that as these protests spread out across the world, they became nomads, gypsies who preserve their ancient knowledge in the form of the mysteries of the deck. And so the tradition developed of the gypsy fortune teller who engaged in divination by the use of cards. The 52 cards of our common deck today are vestiges of the ancient teret pack. The images have evolved from the original pictographs going back only a few centuries, the symbols of the minor arcana. Originally, fifty six cards have changed from Swarens to Spade's, from ones to clubs, from clubs to hearts and from pentacles to diamonds. Although the terror deck is still used for fortune telling today, its higher and more important purpose, according to tradition, was to preserve in symbolic form the laws of the universe as they were known to the ancient adepts. It is this symbolic value of the twenty two cards of the major arcana of the terror attack that we draw on in the system of natural healing.

As we shall see, the symbolism of a particular tarot card resonates with other forces and substances that are important to the person for whom that card represents his or her total essence. We shall begin our introduction of the system by describing the numerological procedures that are used to determine a person's tarot card. Name number. The first component in determining your key numbers and deterrent system is the number derived from your name as it appears on your birth certificate. Your name number is determined by using your full name, first, middle and family names exactly as it was given to you at your birth, if junior or second or third appeared on your birth certificate. This should be included as well, spelled out fully. Even if you have never really used your full name as it appears on your birth certificate or if you have stopped using it, it is this name that represents a matrix of energy which was imprisoned within the imagery of your name and its numerological equivalent at the moment of your birth.

You may feel that your name has very little to do with who you are, but it is possible that even before your birth, you may have had an influence on what name was given to you. While you were in your mother's womb, you were capable of telepathic communication with your parents and may have played a part. While you were in your mother's womb, you were capable of telepathically communicating with your parents and may have played a part in deciding what name was selected for you. Because a tiered system is based on Kabbalistic numerology, you will need to use the Hebrew Kabbalistic alphabet to find the number that corresponds to your name. The twenty two characters of the Hebrew alphabet each have corresponding numbers in translating this alphabet into its English equivalent, you will note that some numbers correspond to more than one letter and that some correspond to combinations of letters that represent a single letter constants in the archaic Hebrew alphabet. One equals two equals to three equals to G. Four equals to five equals to E, six equals to you re and W seven equals to Z, eight equals to H and not equals to the ten equals to I, J and Y. Equals to C and K. Twelve equals to 13 equals to M, fourteen equals to N, fifteen equals to X, 16 equals to O. 17 equals to F. And P.. 18 equals two and. Nineteen equals to Q twenty equals to our twenty, one equals to us, twenty two equals to T. Arrange your name in a vertical column, first middle and last names, and find a number equivalent for each letter or combination of letters when indicated above.

The total of all the numbers corresponding to the letters in your name is your name number. For example, the name John Abell Peterson would look like this J equals a 10 O equals to 16 H equals to eight and equals to 14. Being equal to forty eight in total equals to one. Being equals to two equals to five equals to 12. And they add up to 20. P equals to 17 equals to five, T equals to twenty two equals to five, R equals to 20 s equals to twenty one oh equals to sixteen and equals to fourteen, which all add up to one hundred and twenty. Twenty plus forty eight plus one hundred and twenty equals one hundred and eighty eight, which is equal to the name number. Berth number next, find your birth number, rewriting the numbers corresponding to your birth date in a vertical column. If John Abell Peterson was born on September seven, nineteen thirty one, his birth number would look like this nine seven one nine three one. Equals to 30 in total, which equals to the birth number. So number and soul essence. The first essential quality derived in the system is a phone number, which is then translated into the sole essence to determine the phone number and the birth number and the name number.

Using the same example, the phone number for John Abell Peterson would be one hundred and eighty eight plus 30 equals two hundred and eighteen. In determining the soul essence and also the mental essence, physical essence and diagnostic number below, any number above twenty two must be reduced because there are only 20 to 30 cards used in the system, thus using our example. So the number equals two hundred and eighteen. So essence equals two plus one plus eight, which equals to 11. As you will see when you refer to pages one hundred and sixty nine hundred and thirty four, tarot card number 11 is justice. So the sole essence of John Abell Peterson is represented by the symbolism of justice.

The sole essence is the power, the energy with which you are born into the world, it reflects your purpose in life, the function of your soul, this essence exists whether you manifest it or not. It is your toolbox, the potential that is reflected in your ray. If after adding the digits of the social number together, you still get a number over twenty two advantages of the new number together until we get a number under twenty three. If the phone number has a zero in it, then the digits are added and zero is thrown out, for example, so no one more than three reduces to four one plus zero plus three, not 13. But if the number is one hundred and forty eight, then the sole SS will be one plus four plus eight, which is equal to 13. Mental essence, now we drive the mental essence, subtract the soul essence from the soul, no, then divide by nine because everything is in circles of nine in the system. Therefore, two hundred and eighteen minus 11 divided by nine equals twenty three. The resulting number should always be a whole number if you get a fraction. You made an error in your arithmetic because twenty three is above 20 to reduce by adding the digits, two plus three equals to five, which equals to mental essence.

The mental essence is the directing force of your mind and will, in this case, it is expressed by card number five, the Hierophant. Physical essence. The symbolic number for physical essence is obtained by adding the constant one for one expressive act to the mental essence. In our example, mental essense plus one, therefore five plus one equals six. The physical SS number refers to the actual expression you give to your energy. Obviously, this may differ from the expression proposed by your mind and will. In our example, the physical SS is represented by number six, the LOVERS'. Total essence or diagnostic, no. Your total SS is obtained by adding together the symbolic numbers of the soul, the mind and the body, therefore 11 plus five plus six equals twenty two, which is a total SS or diagnostic number. In our example, then, the diagnostic numbers are presented by number 20 to the full.

All the therapeutics connected with the full in the discussion that follows would serve as preventive guidelines for John Abell Peterson. Because one aspect of your being is mind, your body may be more developed or active than the others, it does no harm to keep in mind the corresponding tarot card for each element. However, the discussion of the individual tarot cards in this chapter refers only to the cards for the total essence or diagnostic number for each individual. Variations, in addition to determining the card that represents your total essence based on your soul essence, mental chapters and physical essence, you can derive further insight into the influences of each state by determining your daily total essence. Suppose today's date is October 14th. Nineteen seventy nine derive a date number as you did for your birth number. One plus zero plus one plus four plus one plus nine plus seven plus nine equals to thirty two, which is your date number.

Add this new date number to your diagnostic number, twenty two in our example, thirty two plus twenty two equals to fifty for. Because this is over twenty three, we add the digits, five plus four equals to nine, which is a new diagnostic number for ten fourteen nineteen seventy nine. Thus, for October 14, nineteen seventy nine, John Abell, Peterson may use card number nine, the Hermit, as his diagnostic card if he wishes for people whose diagnostic cards are very broad in their application. Number 10, the Wheel of Fortune, for example, can be particularly helpful to work with a new diagnostic number for a specific day. Some people go through a distinct rebirth during the Book of their lives, sometimes even more than one, although you keep the same name number throughout your life, you would determine a new birth number and hence a new soul essence, mental essence, physical essence and total essence or diagnostic. No. By taking the date on which you experience your rebirth as your new birth date. Such rebirths are not uncommon in my counseling work.

I sometimes see an individual in whose energy fields I observe a growth pattern that indicates that they have gone through a drastic stage in which they transcended everything they had previously been expressing in their lives. They can then be given a new birth number corresponding to the date on which that graduation took place, and an astrologer can make a new natal chart based on that new date, as well as the time and place where the graduation occurred. Such new birth numbers and natal charts will reflect the drastic changes that have taken place in these people's lives, the new set of tools they're now working with. The twenty two cards of the major arcana.

The total essence, no, or diagnostic number that you have determined by the procedure just described above refers to the corresponding tarot card because there are only twenty two cards. The numbers must be twenty two or less than twenty two cards are listed below with their symbolic meanings. One magician, it represents the truth. Too high priestess, it represents wisdom. Three Empress, it represents authority, unlove. For the emperor, it represents authority on world processes.

Don't miss out!

Visit the website below and you can sign up to receive emails whenever SADANAND PUJARI publishes a new book. There's no charge and no obligation.

https://books2read.com/r/B-A-YJFBB-DVSZC

BOOKS2READ

Connecting independent readers to independent writers.

Also by SADANAND PUJARI

Master The Psychology Of Weight Loss Via Hypnosis Build Healthy Sleep Habits Learn The Art Of Meditation Improve People Management And Build Employee Engagement
Content Marketing Masterclass Create Content That Sells Cyber Security For Normal People Protect Yourself Online Kanban Fundamentals How To Become Insanely Productive
Positive Psychology Art Therapy: Certified Training Bookkeeping In Quickbooks Online (Bookkeeping & Accounting)
Business Impact of Digital Transformation Technologies Learn How to Protect & Restore Yourself from Negative Energy